TIBETAN RESCUE

TIBETAN RESCUE

The Extraordinary Quest
To Save The
Sacred Art Treasures
of Tibet

PAM LOGAN

TUTTLE PUBLISHING
Boston • Rutland, Vermont • Tokyo

This edition published in 2002 by Tuttle Publishing, an imprint of Periplus Editions (HK) Ltd., with editorial offices at 153 Milk Street, Boston, Massachusetts 02109.

Library of Congress Cataloging-in-Publication Data
Logan, Pamela
    Tibetan rescue / Pamela Logan
    p. cm.
    includes index.
    ISBN 0-8048-3421-0 (hc)
    1. Mural painting and decoration, Buddhist—Conservation and restoration—China—Tibet. 2 Dpal-'bar Dgon-pa (Tibet), China) 3. Dpal-spuçs Dgon-pa (Tibet, China) 4. Temples, Buddhist—Conservation and restoration—China—Tibet. I. Title

ND2849.T5 L64 2002
751.6'2'09515—dc21   2001035137

Distributed by

North America,
Latin America, Europe
Tuttle Publishing
Distribution Center
Airport Industrial Park
364 Innovation Drive
North Clarendon, VT 05759-9436
Tel: (802) 773-8930
Toll free tel: (800) 526-2778
Fax: (802) 773-6993
Toll free fax: (800) 329-8885

Japan
Tuttle Publishing
RK Building, 2nd Floor
2-13-10 Shimo-Meguro, Meguro-Ku
Tokyo 153 0064
Tel: (03) 5437 0171
Fax: (03)5437 0755

Asia Pacific
Berkeley Books LTD
130 Joo Seng Road
#06-01/03
Olivine Building
Singapore 368357
Tel: (65) 280-1330
Fax: (65) 280-6290

07 06 05 04 03 02   9 8 7 6 5 4 3 2 1

Printed in the United States of America

Designed by Gopa & Ted2

Contents

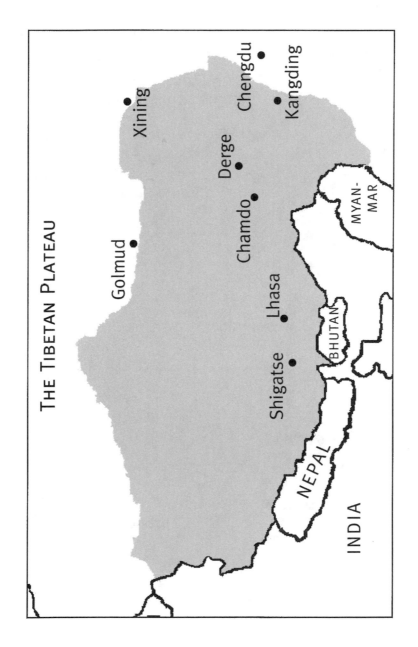

The Tibetan Plateau

Golmud

Xining

Derge

Chamdo

Chengdu

Kangding

Lhasa

Shigatse

NEPAL

BHUTAN

INDIA

MYAN-MAR

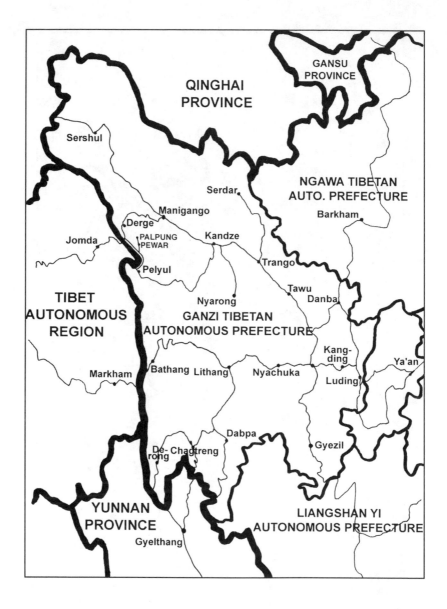

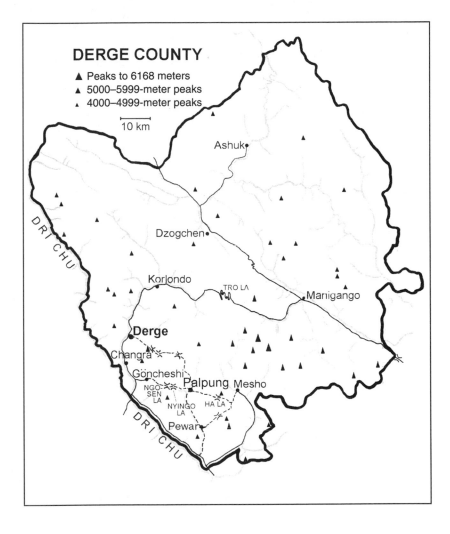

DERGE COUNTY

▲ Peaks to 6168 meters
▲ 5000–5999-meter peaks
▴ 4000–4999-meter peaks

10 km

Ashuk

Dzogchen

Korlondo

TRO LA

Manigango

Derge

Changra

Goncheshi

NGO-SEN LA

Palpung Mesho

NYINGO LA   HA LA

Pewar

DRI CHU

DRI CHU

First Mission: 1994

CHAPTER 1

ENTERING PEWAR and gazing straight up into its lantern, you face *Vajrad-hara*, "holder of the thunderbolt." He is the Primordial Buddha, and represents the pure Buddha-nature from whom all Buddhas arise. His skin is sapphire blue; he sits in tranquil repose in the diamond posture. The *vajra* (double scepter) in his right hand and the *ghanta* (bell) in his left symbolize wisdom and skillful means united. His hands cross gracefully in front of his heart to form a HUM-sound gesture, the final syllable of Om Mani Padme Hum, the sacred song of Tibet.

A Nyingma verse of praise reads: "Master of all-pervasive pristine awareness, unmoving great of dharmata, unsurpassed treasure of wishing jewels; homage to the great Vajradhara!"

August 19

Derge! For three years I yearned to come back to this place, and now, after much waiting and planning and struggling, at last I was here. The truck that brought me rumbled away. Standing at the edge of the highway, I slapped dust from my road-worn clothes and backpack. Then I straightened up and looked around.

The town had changed. Its streets now had pavement, not the soupy mud I remembered. They clattered with a familiar chaos of logging trucks and horses, vendors and monks, townspeople and itinerate herdsmen. On the main thoroughfare, brick and concrete buildings coalesced under the busy hands of Chinese workers; yet much of the town was still

I

covered in old-fashioned Tibetan timber houses. Flowers bloomed from pots on the balconies, where I saw women in traditional dress taking down laundry. Over it all floated the sweet smell of summer mountains.

I shouldered my backpack and set out toward the county guest house. A gang of monks loitering by the side of the street spotted me. "Hey! Hello! Nihao! Okay!" they teased. I smiled and passed on.

At the guest house I dropped my baggage, then came back outside to the street. There were monks everywhere, hundreds of them. Some kind of Buddhist rite must be going on, I thought. I asked a passerby where I could find the lama Pewar Rinpoche, and was directed to Gönchen Gonpa, a large Sakya sect monastery at the town's southern edge.

The path to Gönchen was a rough dirt road paralleling a little stream. Hundreds of people, many of them monks, were walking the same way. Swept along by the foaming sea of faithful, I came through the stone portal and entered the temple courtyard.

Inside, the place was jammed. I asked someone where to find Pewar Rinpoche and the man pointed to a doorway across the courtyard. "He'll be coming right out," the man said. "Wait here."

So I waited. The ceremony, a Wheel of Time Initiation, was about to resume. Monks were going into the temple, while lay-people remained in the courtyard to catch whatever karmic overflow might come drifting through the doors. A couple of Public Security Bureau officers were there, too, eyeing the crowds and keeping a close watch on the officiating lama, who was, someone told me, a Tibetan exile from India. I was happily snapping pictures of the proceedings when one of the policemen spotted me. He pushed his way though the crowds to where I was standing. At first speechless, he looked me up and down.

"Come with me," he said finally, and led me out to the street.

We went to the police headquarters, a tumbledown relic emblazoned with the now-dated slogan, "Long Live Mao Zedong Thought." Upstairs, I was given a strong cup of jasmine tea. The officer was called Malu, a Tibetan, and he was head of the foreign affairs division. Responding to his questions in my bad Chinese, I explained who I was and brought out my travel papers. That made everything all right. After I had been duly entered in his black registration book, and we had fetched my baggage, he led me through the narrow, twisted pathways of Derge's Old Town, to Pewar Rinpoche's house on the top tier.

Two monks distributing sanctified yarn and kusha *stalks are mobbed by the faithful attending a Kalachakra empowerment at Gönchen Monastery.*

Pewar Rinpoche was the leader of Pewar Monastery, one of the two monasteries I was coming to look at and, ultimately, repair. So far, the project was not going according to plan. I wasn't supposed to be here alone; I was supposed to be part of a team led by my friend and mentor, Wong How Man. A Hong Kong native, Wong was a veteran of expeditions on the Tibetan plateau and to the farthest reaches of China; it was he who conceived of this monastery conservation program. We were supposed to have with us a couple of experts in repairing ancient buildings. The journey should have been made in a deluxe, tricked-out Land Rover, not as I had done, by hitchhiking in an antique Dongfeng truck.

I had come from Chengdu, capital of Sichuan Province. Although

Derge[1] is culturally Tibetan, China draws provincial boundaries so as to enclose it within Sichuan Province, and indeed Derge is more easily reached from Chengdu than from Lhasa, the Tibetan capital. Tibetans, however, see things differently. To them, the province containing Derge is Kham, a fuzzy geographic entity that includes large portions of Sichuan and Tibetan Autonomous Region and a snippet of northwest Yunnan. Depending on your point of view, I had traveled over eastern Kham or western Sichuan to get here. Either way, that meant six high passes and nearly one thousand teeth-rattling kilometers of rugged, sparsely populated terrain.

Our plans had been bollixed by a major snafu that occurred in Chengdu as the team was preparing to leave. We are were all there: the leader Wong, a conservation architect named John Sanday, and Razat, his Nepalese assistant. We had Wong's fancy car, a driver, and had purchased needed supplies. In Derge and along the way, people were expecting us. Everything was set.

But Derge was a closed area, forbidden to foreigners unless they had special permits. In the past, as a vagabond tourist, I had always finessed this point by allowing myself to be kicked out of closed areas, a process that took about as much time as it did to sightsee a town. Now, I was part of a genuine team of "foreign experts," and we were doing things the legal way. We had an official host, the Sichuan Nationalities Research Institute. They had duly received all our particulars several months before. But after arriving in Chengdu we learned that someone had gone on vacation with our paperwork left sitting on his desk. The permit process required many approvals, and not even the first document had been stamped. Nevertheless, the Institute promised that our permits would be ready in a few days' time.

"A few days" turned into a week, then two. Wong had urgent business back in Hong Kong, so he departed, leaving me in charge. Every day I went to the Institute's office, but all they had for me were vague promises.

---

1 "Derge" is the spelling most often seen in the West, but the R is not pronounced by natives of the region, who say the word so as to rhyme it with *reggae*. Letter-by-letter transliteration of the Tibetan yields "sDe dGe," which is unpronounceable except to specialists. The Pinyinized Chinese name is Dege. I will follow the following rule of thumb for place names: predominantly Tibetan places will be named in Tibetan, with Chinese name following in parentheses on first use. Predominantly Chinese places will be named in Chinese. Please see Appendix IV for a table of toponyms in both languages.

Despite the fact that most of them were minorities and some of them were Tibetan, they weren't much interested in our project. I phoned up Wong's influential friends and begged them for help, but they could do nothing. At the height of Chengdu's torrid summer, the whole city seemed asleep.

On August 7th, after nearly three weeks, we gave up. The experts, John and Razat, had other work to do. Back in his Hong Kong head-quarters, Wong concurred, saying that if we accept this mistreatment from our hosts, our face will suffer irreparable harm. We decided that the two experts would pull out. John and Razat got on the plane for home, leaving me to carry on alone.

Welcome to the frustrations of working in Tibet. If it wasn't bad enough that Tibet is poor, it's worse that you can't even help without permission from a dozen reluctant authorities. That's because the Chinese government, xenophobic even in the best of times, considers Tibetan areas to be extremely sensitive. They assume that foreigners are going there not to help so much as to foment rebellion among Tibetans against their Chinese rulers. If we're not spies for the Dalai Lama, then we must be journalists inves-tigating human rights. You can't blame them for being suspicious, given the outrage that inflames the West about China's treatment of Tibetans and the number of visitors who have published highly critical reports.

Our monastery project had the saving grace of being initiated by a Hong Kong native, which went a long way toward allaying Chinese sus-picions. But even with that advantage, we had an uphill road ahead.

So here I was, shorn of my team, bent on doing what I could to move the project forward. Malu took me to Pewar Rinpoche's house, a three-story fortification erected on the side of a steep hill overlooking the town. The house had an attached temple and a workroom upstairs where a lad sat all day carving sutra printing plates. I was given a small, plain chamber that opened onto an upstairs terrace.

An hour later, the tulku[2] himself returned. I heard a bell clanging as

2 Tulkus, or incarnate lamas, are sometimes called "Living Buddhas" in the West, a mislead-ing and erroneous term. Tibetan Buddhists hold them to be emanations of deities or important historical personages who have become so advanced that their powers are carried forward in successive reincarnations. Selection is made using indications left by the past incarnation, or clues appearing in dreams of prominent lamas, or by divination.

the courtyard gate opened, and then the clump-clump-clump of the lama and his entourage ascending the steep wooden stairs. A portly figure swathed in maroon cloth burst into the sitting room. Seeing me, he laughed with delight. On outward-turning feet he tottered across the room and collapsed windily onto his throne-like chair. The steward rushed up to pour butter-tea for him into a jade bowl.

"Hello, hello!" he giggled in high-pitched English. I tried to answer him in Tibetan, as I knew his Chinese was limited and his English even more so, but the words got knotted up inside my throat and I could only sit there and grin. In the end, the policeman Malu, who had been waiting with me, had to remind him who I was.

I had met the lama[3] in Chengdu a few years before, introduced by my mentor Wong. The lama's waddling gait, yellow singlet, purple monk's skirt, and long dyed hair worn in a topknot had seemed an amazing anachronism in that teaming city. He was about 60, with a playful personality that belied acute intelligence. "Thank you very much!" he would say to me, giggling in English; but behind that mild exterior were facets polished to a diamond hardness. His words carried a lot of weight in this town.

Monks of the Sakya order are not compelled to remain celibate, and it's murmured that Pewar Rinpoche has a wife stashed somewhere, and perhaps even a girlfriend or two. But this I never saw. What I did see were throngs of followers and friends who were utterly devoted to him.

That evening, I ate yak sausage and drank salt tea from a porcelain bowl while Pewar Rinpoche sat on his throne receiving visitors. It was a considerable climb to reach this house; nevertheless the tulku had plenty of callers. Townspeople appeared, one after the other, bent low in the doorway, eyes humble but full of love and hope. He conversed with jovial friends, listened sympathetically to tales of woe, dispensed uplifting counsel, applied his sacred handprints where requested to a painting, and gave out envelopes of herbs that had been blessed. The people came away with tears in their eyes, transformed. As the evening progressed, a pile of

---

3   Pewar Rinpoche, whose full name is Pewar Chimay Dorje, is actually twice-incarnate, for in addition to the title Pewar, he is also the fourth in a line of emanations associated with Are Monastery.

tattered bills the color of autumn leaves grew on the table. I decided that tulku-hood must be a good living in this town.

Pewar Rinpoche.

My marching orders were: once in Derge I should seek out a man called Shongshong,[4] a Tibetan builder who would work with us on the monastery restoration project. I had only to mention his name for someone to go running out to fetch him. After dinner he appeared: a down-to-earth fellow in a plain khaki-colored Tibetan robe, 53 years old, with a bald pate and monkishly short hair.

I held out my hand for Shongshong to shake, which seemed to surprise him. He unbent from his stooped posture and grasped it quickly, looking at the floor all the while. Then he took a seat on a low stool—much lower than the couch I was sitting on. The steward poured Shongshong some

4 In Kham, childhood nicknames occasionally follow people to adulthood, and so it was with this man.

7

butter-tea, but he hardly looked at it. He seemed overcome with emotion.

"Your journey must have been hard. Thank you so much for coming!" he said in Chinese in a low, fervent voice. His head was slightly bowed; his eyes glanced furtively around the room, rarely turning far in enough in their sockets to meet mine. "You are generous to come to Derge, and to help us. We are very grateful that foreign experts are willing to repair our monasteries. I'm sorry that this place is poor; conditions are so bad. . . ."

Shongshong.

He went on in this vein for some minutes, while I tried to reassure him that the journey wasn't so bad, that I love Derge and I really *wanted* to come. His abject appreciation was embarrassing. We hadn't done anything yet, and already they were grateful! I didn't want to think how impossibly ambitious this program was, and how dismal its chances for success.

The monastery conservation program was conceived by Wong How Man, who, over the years, traveled a great deal in western Sichuan and knew of the area's rich architectural heritage. He met conservation architect John Sanday, who was then employed by the Getty Grant Fund. John had lived and worked in Nepal for many years and was a devoted fan of Tibetan buildings. With the help of his inside advocacy, the Getty agreed to fund a preliminary survey as a first step.

The survey expedition took place in April, 1991. Wong and a Belgian architect named Patrick Troch, escorted by a phalanx of officials, came to western Sichuan by car caravan. Their original goal was conservation of the Derge Printing House, a famous landmark in the region. However, by the time Wong and Troch arrived, the Derge Printing House was already being restored by the government. Accordingly, Wong and Troch reverted to the second goal of the mission: a search for other architectural masterpieces in need of repair.

The team surveyed a total of eighteen monasteries. They investigated history, economics and lineage, drew up floor plans, and noted carefully the condition of major buildings. The result was an exhaustive report that I helped edit after the mission was over. I also helped write a grant proposal to the Getty to fund the next phase. It was during those long nights polishing text, arranging illustrations, and transliterating Tibetan script that I earned my place on the next field team.

Wong and Troch ended up selecting two monasteries for future conservation. They were Pewar and Palpung Monasteries,[5] both of which I had visited during my own solo travels. Palpung was much the showier of the two monasteries: its spectacular main temple was said to be second only to Lhasa's Potala Palace in size. Pewar was much smaller, but because it held marvelous and rare murals, they took it on as a satellite project.

Alas, John Sanday left the Getty to return to his practice in Kathmandu. Our proposal was flaky and far-fetched; without an insider backing it, the Getty lost interest. Wong and I and the rest of the team watched three years slip past as we searched for another donor. Then, in

---

5   During Wong's initial survey, the only names he recorded for the two monasteries were the Chinese names "Baiya" and "Babang." Subsequently I was able to obtain the names written in Tibetan script, which transliterate to "Pewar" and "Palpung." Yet all of these spellings are misleading when it comes to pronunciation. The best Romanization I can come up with that's consistent with local pronunciation is "Beh-yah" and "Beh-bung." (The initial sound is between a P and a B, and thus cannot be rendered accurately in our alphabet.)

1993 an earthquake hit Derge that caused a part of Palpung to collapse. Suddenly the matter seemed much more urgent, and Wong stepped up his fund-raising. In the spring of 1994, a breakthrough arrived in the form of a $25,000 grant from the Mongolian and Tibetan Affairs Commission of Taiwan.[6] Out of this grant had come the considerable expenses of our Chengdu fiasco, and it would pay for our now-rescheduled expedition in the fall.

I had signed onto this project for the chance to come back to Derge, a place I had fallen in love with. I never thought it would be my responsibility to make the project work, and I never thought about the likelihood—and consequences—of failure. Now I saw the real people who were depending on Wong and me. The project was so huge, so difficult. Shongshong's gratitude made me feel terribly guilty. What if we failed?

When we reached the end of Shongshong's speech of thanks, and my ardent protestations, we could talk business. He asked: "Why is there only you? Where are the other experts?"

In my rocky Chinese, I told him the saga of our permits. He nodded, unhappy but accepting. The senseless behavior of Chinese officialdom enraged us foreigners; but to Shongshong, God, fate and government were all facets of the same impenetrable mechanism, and anger was pointless. We discussed the journey to Pewar and Palpung and what we would do there. The details were quickly settled.

For the rest of the evening, Shongshong sat on his stool, saying little. He was obviously content merely to be near Pewar Rinpoche. His mien was honest, humble, and deeply devout. I would almost have called him a simple peasant, but I knew he was no dummy, for he had masterminded repairs to the Derge Printing House, the prefecture's most important Tibetan monument. That had been a huge and complex job, lasting years.

I wished Shongshong would drop the exaggerated respect, because I felt like a complete fraud coming with nothing more than good intentions and a camera. Everyone was deeply disappointed that the long-awaited

6 As China's "government-in-exile," the Republic of China maintains this ministry in preparation for its hoped-for return to the mainland, and also to look after the needs of Mongolians and Tibetans resident on Taiwan island.

experts hadn't come. All I could tell them was that the mission was postponed until fall, but that I had come to take photographs and get information that would help John Sanday prepare for it. Outwardly, I was confident, but in my heart I wondered if this project could ever fly.

However, there was one thing to be glad for: now, at least, I could give up worrying, roll up my sleeves, and do some real work.

CHAPTER 2

IN PEWAR'S lantern are four panels devoted to the *Great Sakya Patriarchs*. One of them, known as Sakya Pandita, brought Buddhism to Mongolia. In 1244, Godan Khan, grandson of Jenghis, summoned the 62-year-old lama, for he wished to receive Buddhist teachings from the venerated master. The old Tibetan dared not refuse—not with the powerful Mongolian army sitting at Tibet's doorstep. His journey from the Tibetan plateau to the Mongolian capital took three years. Because of this heroic mission, the Mongols became patrons of Tibet's Buddhist faith. To this day, Tibetan Buddhism is still practiced in Mongolia.

While in the Khan's court, Sakya Pandita continued his relentless philosophic inquiry. He wrote not only about Buddhism, but also prescribed everyday advice for correct living according to the Eightfold Path. One verse reads:

> The more you desire to be exalted,
> The more you should endeavor to be useful to others.
> Do not those who want to wash their faces
> Need first to wipe the mirror clean?

August 23

I had to wait three days in Derge for the Wheel of Time ceremony to be over before the devout Shongshong would consider leaving town. On the day of departure, a jeep took us to the trailhead at a village called Göncheshi (Chinese: Anjihei), an hour down the Sichuan-Tibet highway.

Although Göncheshi had no telephone, Shongshong somehow arranged for a local man and two horses to materialize for us there. Together we rode into the mountains, over nGosen La (4600 meters, 15,092 feet) and Nyingo La (4270 meters, 14,009 feet), on a trail that throbbed with memories from three years earlier.

Palpung Monastery and surroundings.

My entry into Palpung—on horseback, accompanied by Shongshong and an attendant—contrasted sharply with that of the soggy, footsore waif who showed up on the doorstep in 1991. Then, I had walked that trail, accompanied by five Tibetan pilgrims I met on the way in. They were making a two-day circumambulation of Palpung, a Buddhist pilgrimage. That trek was the hardest walk of my life: climbing to high pastures, navigating slippery precipices, being pelted by rain, and spending the night in a nomad's tent before finally reaching the monastery.

All of this Tibet business was a radical departure from my original life's plan. As a kid growing up in the Chicago suburbs, I wanted to be a scientist and spent hours peering at the stars. Thanks to the encouragement of my parents, I did well enough to be admitted to Caltech as an undergraduate, although I quickly flunked out of astronomy and changed to engineering. From there, I went on to graduate school at Stanford, where I earned a Ph.D. in aerospace. Afterwards I spent three postdoc years at UCLA, working in a combustion lab and teaching classes in fluid dynamics.

This conventional, academic-track career was derailed by a 1986 vacation trip to Nepal. There, while trekking in the Himalayas, I heard of people called Khampas—men of Kham—reputed to be the fiercest warriors in Tibet. As a long-time practitioner of martial arts, I was fascinated by the Khampas.[7] But Kham was ruled by China and strictly off limits to foreigners. I could only fantasize about going there.

A few years after that Nepal trip, I learned about travel grants available from a southern California nonprofit called the Durfee Foundation. They had an outlandish program, the American-Chinese Adventure Capital Program, that invited Caltech alumni to dream up personal China quests. I wrote a proposal saying I wanted to go to Kham in search of warriors. A few weeks later they sent back a letter saying yes.

Nothing has been the same since.

While getting ready for my warrior quest, I met Wong How Man and joined his organization, the China Exploration and Research Society, or CERS. In Wong's long career, he had traveled extensively in Kham and knew the area well. The monastery conservation program, which was then in the planning stages, would be smack-dab in the middle of Kham's cultural heart. It would be administered by CERS, then based in Los Angeles where we both lived.

CERS was a small organization, patterned in spirit (if not in budget) after the National Geographic Society. It was peopled by an eccentric band of explorers, Sinophiles, and prominent Chinese Americans. In those early days, our newsletter was typed on a manual typewriter, and our main annual event was a barbecue in Wong's backyard.

Like other members of CERS, I was captivated by the romance of Wong How Man's incredible vocation: exploring China's exotic frontiers. He hunted in the Pamirs with Kyrgyz using their trained eagles, and he

---

7 In Tibetan, the suffix *pa* indicates a person, so a Khampa is a person (usually a man) of Kham, a Gelugpa is an adherent of the Gelug lineage, etc.

documented Lugu Lake's matrilineal Muso villages. He observed wild gibbons in southwestern rainforest, and he rode with fur-hatted Manchurians on reindeer-pulled sleds. He sat with Uighurs at prayer in Silk Road mosques, and he led an expedition that discovered a new source for the Yangtze River. Wong's photographs and articles were published in *National Geographic*. The man was a genius at promoting his work and attracting sponsors. Now he was beginning a major program in western Sichuan—the very place that I, the terrified novice, wanted to go.

Wong How Man, at Tuotuohe on the Golmud-Lhasa highway.

Naturally, I begged Wong to take me along. On my own, I would need to hitchhike, dodge police checkpoints, and communicate in Tibetan or Chinese. With him, I could ride in a Land Cruiser, be listed on a travel permit, and have English-speaking people around me all of the time. But Wong had more important priorities than my travel aspirations. I was just a wannabe with no relevant skills, an unproven commodity that could barely even speak Mandarin. He couldn't justify me to his Chinese hosts and was reluctant to pester them. I could hardly blame him.

So I went alone. His trip was three weeks; mine lasted months. I managed to get around Kham on my own, visiting sixteen counties, including several places Wong had included in his survey. By the time I returned home, Tibetan Sichuan had imprinted deep into my psyche. Plus, now I was experienced. Working with Wong on his monastery conservation project was the obvious next step. And now, finally, Wong was glad to have me on board.

So here I was, declaring to all and sundry that I was going to repair and conserve Pewar and Palpung Monasteries. Naively, I thought that they would immediately approve my plans for conservation, and bend over backwards to cooperate, both with me and with one another. I soon found out that things are not quite so straightforward as that.

At Pewar Monastery, it was true: they were desperately glad to have us and would do anything we asked. Its lineage, the Sakya, was dominant in Derge, and so Pewar Rinpoche had a lot of influence, could host me well and get things done. Although he didn't live at Pewar, he was not far away and clearly in charge.

Palpung was a completely different matter. It belonged to a different lineage—Kagyu—so it had no strong base in Derge town. To them, Pewar was an insignificant neighbor, and the two monasteries had no relationship to speak of. Instead, Palpung's network extended to other Kagyu monasteries, especially the order's chief monastery, Tsurphu, which lay more than a thousand kilometers away. Palpung's ruling incarnate lama lived in exile and had little to do with his monastery's day-to-day affairs. Nevertheless, the monks of Palpung held him in high esteem. It was necessary, therefore, that we obtain this tulku's approval for our proposed project. We were also hoping he would contribute some of his rumored vast wealth to it. Luckily enough, just before Wong and I and the others left Hong Kong for what turned out to be an aborted mission, we got a chance to ask.

Kenting Yamthong Myutsi Goshir Tai Situ, or "Great lama who leads all beings of the universe to ultimate peace and who gives empowerments to the crown of the emperor and who possesses great loving kindness," is known as Situ Rinpoche for short. The current Situ Rinpoche is twelfth in the line of incarnate lamas bearing that name, having been identified while still an infant and enthroned at Palpung in 1955 at the age of eighteen months. He came from a family of farmers in Pelyul (Baiyu), in the southern part of the Derge Kingdom. At the age of six he was brought out of his homeland and into exile, fleeing to Bhutan and eventually India along with thousands of other Tibetans. Despite being in exile, at age twenty-one he assumed his traditional responsibilities as one of the foremost leaders of the Karma Kagyu order.

The Tai Situpas have enjoyed comparatively good relations with their Chinese neighbors. The line, which is said to be an emanation of Maitreya, the Buddha of the Future, passed through Marpa the Translator and is said to have included one Chinese emperor, Tai Shen Chey. The first Situ Rinpoche ever to be called by that name, Chokyi Gyaltsen, received the title from the Ming Dynasty emperor Yong Le in 1407.

Now a man of great power in the world Buddhist community, the Twelfth Situ Rinpoche has returned to the Tibetan plateau several times. During a 1991 visit to Derge, he attracted a reported 30,000 people seeking public initiation and blessing. At Palpung, he led a two-month empowerment that was attended by 1,835 monks and nuns, and he ordained 1,200 students. Outside Tibet, too, the Tai Situpa is venerated. He lives a peripatetic life, bouncing between groups of devotees scattered among Buddhist centers worldwide.

We went to have an audience with Situ Rinpoche at the Karma Kagyu Buddhist Center, located in an apartment building in Hong Kong's seedy Wan Chai district. The door was opened by a blonde American woman who ushered us through the temple room, past its glittering shrine, to a chamber in the rear.

His Eminence sat in an armchair, his back ramrod straight, robes neatly arranged, mien kingly calm. His bearing took me aback for a moment; I stumbled through the greeting protocol until, to my relief, he waved us into chairs. People of various hues glided in carrying trays laid with immaculate teacups, cream, and sugar. It was altogether different from the Tibetan hospitality I was used to: butter-tea swimming in a chipped porcelain bowl and a haunch of dried yak proffered along with a foot-long silver-handled knife.

Although I am a Buddhist, my inclinations are toward Zen and away from the elaborate mysticism of Tibet. My science training makes reincarnation hard to swallow. But I can't deny that incarnate lamas have formidable wisdom and charisma. After all, they are painstakingly selected as toddlers from good, devout, and usually prosperous families. The boys are nurtured with extraordinary care in a monastic setting in which they are treated like gods. At the same time, they learn discipline and humility through a rigorous spiritual education. It's no wonder that tulkus turn out to be remarkable adults.

Situ Rinpoche was handsome in a neat, square-jawed sort of way. His eyes scanned and analyzed and took in everything. He seemed utterly without self-doubt. Wong How Man, the program leader, was supposed to do the talking, but even he, normally a genius in public relations, couldn't seem to find his voice. We listened respectfully while Situ Rinpoche held forth on Palpung Monastery, his childhood home and traditional seat.

"Palpung was a center of learning, famous throughout Tibet," he told us in businesslike, Tibetan-accented English. "Before 1950, it had over one thousand monks. After 1959, the Chinese closed the monastery and sent the monks home. Many monasteries were completely destroyed during the Cultural Revolution,[8] but Palpung was saved because villagers moved into the temple. The government had offices, storehouses, and a medical clinic there. The shrine room was a piggery. . . ."

At this notion his eyes laughed and a bemused smile momentarily softened his mouth. He continued: "Currently, many monasteries are being repaired, or are being rebuilt if there was nothing left. But not Palpung. So now there are a lot of new buildings that look very clean and beautiful, but Palpung is still in a very bad condition. The people in Derge are simple: they don't see the value of old things; they prefer to have new things. So everyone thinks Palpung is a failure. The monks feel very bad.

8   The Great Proletarian Cultural Revolution occurred in China between 1966 and 1976, driven by Mao's desire to accelerate China's evolution toward an ideal Marxist society. It was a period of intense turmoil and destruction, when all things normally respected in China—schools and educated persons, ancient monuments and books—were attacked by roving gangs of young zealots. Those suspected of ideological impurity were mercilessly persecuted, and many people were killed or committed suicide. Millions suffered from the economic chaos that resulted from the endless political movements.

And of course there is real physical danger from the building collapsing. I cannot allow this to happen.

"This is my monastery, so it is my duty to save it."

In 1984, Situ Rinpoche visited Palpung and donated 100,000 yuan[9] toward purchase of new timber for repairs[10] and another 100,000 yuan for construction of a *shedra* (Buddhist university) above the monastery. He was supportive of our conservation proposal, but he had no more cash to give. I didn't understand it, for his followers always seemed to find the capital needed for construction of faux Tibetan temples in India, Europe, Japan, Taiwan, America—everywhere, it seemed, except Tibet itself, home to hundreds of endangered authentic structures.

Perhaps Situ Rinpoche's problem had something to do with an ugly succession dispute over the identification of a boy who would become Karmapa, leader of the order. It was tragic that while Kagyupas around the world were busy taking sides in this fracas, one of their oldest strongholds—a building which had survived war, weather, and revolution— might be lost. The $25,000 from Taiwan was a drop in the bucket compared to what would ultimately be needed to restore Palpung to its former brilliance. But for now it would have to do.

At Palpung, the monks were eager for news of their beloved leader. Have you seen him? Where is he? What did he say? And, most of all, when is he coming back? The last question I couldn't answer. The monks remembered Wong How Man's visit three years previously, and they knew that he wanted to repair their monastery, but they didn't seem to understand why. I later learned that they thought he was just a devout Chinese Buddhist who was going to pay for repairs as an offering. The vagaries of international fund-raising and architectural conservation were way outside their experience. Three years of silence had left them disap-

9   The exchange rate, which is set by the government, was about 3.2 in 1984. It subsequently rose to 8.1 yuan per U.S. dollar and stayed in that vicinity from 1994 to the program's completion.

10 According Palpung's abbot, the government gave 200,000 yuan for remaking of the great Maitreya statue in the main hall, and 10,000 for emergency repairs following the 1993 earthquake. The monastery itself raised 20,000, and borrowed 70,000 more. By 1994 all this money had been spent.

pointed and confused. That I had come, but without any cash, did little
to assuage their hurt.

Nevertheless, I determinedly set out to accomplish my mission: to
document the current condition of Palpung so that John Sanday could
prepare for a fall expedition.

Three years had passed since Wong's survey, and the monastery's situation had changed. There had been an earthquake the previous year
that had accelerated the building's decay; it shook down the toilet wing,
which had since been replaced.[11] Shongshong showed me around the
main temple and explained its many ills. I took copious photographs and
notes for John Sanday.

In the course of the work, one morning I was passing by the north courtyard when I heard an unexpected sound: a boy upstairs chanting sutras.
The voice was tremulous, breathy: a child struggling to make his unde-
veloped larynx do the job of a resonant bass. In 1991, all the Palpung
monks had been adults, so I was surprised that so small a child would be
here now. The sound was coming from a third-floor room I had not been
shown. The paper-covered lattice windows were closed, hiding the
source. After a minute of listening, I shrugged and went on with my work.

In the afternoon, I passed by again. The chanting had ceased, and the
windows were still closed. But now I saw something that made me stop
in my tracks: a pair of enigmatic almond eyes. They were gazing through
a square of glass in the center of one window panel, a tiny porthole to the
outside world.

I thought: those eyes belong to the chanting child. Novice monks, or
traba, are nothing unusual. I had seen plenty of traba before: mischievous
scamps, running circles around older monks or fidgeting through cere-
monies. But as days went by, it seemed to me that this boy was not an
ordinary traba. He never slid open the lattice to put his head outside or
called to the monks who walked beneath his quarters. He remained in his
high chamber, aloof to the outside world.

Shongshong told me that the boy was five years old and had been dis-

11 In Tibetan buildings, the toilet is usually a tiny upstairs room that protrudes from the main
structure. Palpung's toilet was three stories tall and large, a veritable building in itself.

covered last year on the grasslands not far away. Born of nomad parents, he had been proclaimed to be the living reincarnation of Urgyen Rinpoche,[12] one of four tulkus who traditionally dwell in Palpung. (Situ Rinpoche is the most important of the four). After his discovery, the boy and his family were brought to Palpung, where he was now receiving the best education the monastery could offer. Two older brothers also joined Palpung as traba.

Urgyen Rinpoche gazing from the window of his quarters.

After just one year of study, Urgyen Rinpoche was already reading and writing the complicated Tibetan script, the first step on a long road to the spiritual master he would become. If he was a successful student, he would probably one day lead the monastery, for Palpung's other three tulkus now lived in exile, returning only for rare and brief visits. Their

---

12 The name is challenging to render in our alphabet. It is sometimes spelled "Orgyen" (the R is barely pronounced). Transliteration of the Tibetan gives "Wöngen." In Pinyin, it comes out as "Wengen."

absence left a huge void in Palpung, a void which would be Urgyen Rinpoche's duty to fill.

On my last day at Palpung, Shongshong took me to see the little tulku.
His room was so dark that it was a minute before I could make out the
boy's figure, swathed in maroon cloth and yellow silk. He seemed very
small sitting there on his cushioned platform. His old tutor stood next to
him. His father, dressed in the dark tatters of a herdsman, stood against
the wall along with the two monk brothers. The older boys looked happy
to see me—I was probably interrupting a boring routine. Although nothing had yet been said or done, everyone in the room was beaming. The
source of the glow seemed to be little Urgyen Rinpoche himself.

Over the years I've met several child tulkus. They are remarkable
beings: exceptionally patient, cannily observant, poised far beyond their
years. Living as an object of deep love and veneration had already begun
to shape this child. Although he was too shy to open his mouth in my
presence, he gazed at me with a supernatural combination of boyish
curiosity and fatherly kindness. Prompted by his father, the little tulku
blessed me and presented me with a silver spoon engraved with Tibetan
designs—a token of thanks for my help to his monastery. As I left the
chamber, exiting according to protocol with my head bowed, I felt my
worries dispelled.

CHAPTER 3

TUCKED IN A CORNER beneath one of Pewar's great deities is a small, easily overlooked trio: *a cow, a deer, and a lion*. They could be an allusion to the following parable:

Once upon a time, a rich businessman in Benares hired a herdsman to look after his cattle. The herdsman took the cows to a forest to graze. Every few days he brought back milk and cheese to give to the wealthy owner.

But a lion lived also in that forest, so the cows were nervous and did not give enough milk. When the herdsman went to his master to explain the situation, the master advised: "Capture another animal that is the lion's friend, and rub this animal's fur with poison. When the lion licks his friend, he will die."

So the herdsman captured a small doe which he know to be on good terms with the lion. After rubbing the doe with poison, he waited a few days and then set the animal free. When the lion saw his friend, he was so full of happiness that he abandoned caution and joyfully licked her fur in greeting. Shortly thereafter, the poor lion died.

The moral of the story is: be cautious and not greedy.

That night, as Shongshong and I ate our noodles by candlelight, he told me about his life. "I was born in Derge town," he said, speaking a gentle, iambic cadence that was the Derge dialect of Chinese, Shongshong's second language. "My parents had a mill beside the river. My mother gave birth to ten children, but three died young. My father was very religious, and his faith influenced me as a boy. In 1950, I started at primary school, studying Tibetan and Chinese."

Shongshong's boyhood world must have been full of change, fear, and uncertainty—although he never alluded to his personal suffering. New China came into being when he was seven years old, and by the time he was eight, Lhasa had fallen and Chinese were in possession of virtually all major towns across the Tibetan plateau. At first, Tibetans had high hopes that Communist rule would not be destructive to their traditional way of life. Indeed, in the early years of the 1950s, the Chinese were extremely cautious in introducing changes to the status quo. Tibetans were allowed to live pretty much as they always had, except that now Lhasa's rapacious tax collectors had been put out of business. Tibetans, therefore, were guardedly optimistic that Chinese rule might prove to be acceptable.

As the years went by, however, the Communists grew impatient with the Tibetans' unwillingness to go along with their economic and social reforms. Pressure increased on Tibetans to reorganize their society. One exile reported, "the Communists entered the houses of better class Tibetans and ransacked them; they took the clothes of the masters and made the servants wear them, and the masters were forced to put on the servants' clothes."[13] Promising youngsters were sent to cities such as Chengdu to undergo political indoctrination. Perhaps most ominously, the Chinese began working to unseat the lamas from their traditional positions of authority. Clearly the old social order was going to change.

Tibetan discontent gradually increased. In 1954, the Chinese government ordered people to give up their weapons, a move that aroused furious opposition among gun-loving Khampas. In 1955, the Chinese stepped up the pace of reforms, redistributing land and trying to settle the nomads. They initiated a campaign of persecution against the wealthy, especially those who resisted their new rulers. In 1956, the Derge county government confiscated Shongshong's parents' property and their family milling business. Shongshong left school and moved with his family to the countryside, where they become farmers.

Meanwhile, south of Derge, rebellion was breaking out. A fiery Nyarong woman named Dorje Yudon led an army of Khampas against

13 Chögyam Trungpa, *Born in Tibet*, Shambhala Publications, 1985, p. 157.

Chinese troops.[14] After two months of fierce fighting, her rebel band was forced into the hills to wage what would be a protracted guerrilla campaign. The fighting spread like wildfire as more Khampas joined the Chushi Gangdrug (Four Rivers, Six Ranges) resistance movement. Even the young Derge Prince joined a roving platoon of children who specialized in digging trenches across the highway to hamper Chinese transport.[15]

Tibetan guerrillas attacked Chinese garrisons in Chagtreng (Xiangcheng) and Gyelthang (Zhongdian), which lies in northwest Yunnan. In Lithang (Litang), Chinese soldiers laid a month-long siege to rebels and townspeople sheltering in Lithang Gonpa. Their defense was broken only when the PLA called in an airplane to bomb the monastery.[16]

That year, 1956, marked the beginning of what would turn out to be two decades of devastation. In the course of putting down the Khampa revolt, the Chinese executed ringleaders, arrested thousands more, and razed monasteries. The guerrillas appealed to Lhasa for help, but the vacillating and rudderless Tibetan government was afraid of angering the Chinese and turned a deaf ear.[17]

Meanwhile, tens of thousands of ordinary Tibetans were uprooted by the fighting and by fear that their religion and way of life would be obliterated. They took to the road: bands of ragged travelers with trains of animals, dumping or bartering possessions as they went along, always in terror of meeting a Chinese patrol over the next hill. Food and pasture were in short supply. Many had no real plan for where they were going; but, guided by pilgrim instincts, they headed west, toward Lhasa and the Himalayan passes beyond. The passes led to Buddha's birthplace, a land of imagined succor.

14 Jamyang Norbu, *Horseman in the Snow: The Story of Aten, an Old Khampa Warrior*, Information Office, Central Tibetan Secretariat, Dharamsala, India, 1979, p.106. Also published as *Warriors of Tibet: The Story of Aten and the Khampas Fight for the Freedom of Their Country*, Wisdom Publications, London, 1986.

15 According to Chögyam Trungpa, his mother was ruling Derge as regent in his stead; ultimately she escaped with her ministers. The *Annals of Dege County* tell us that the "last" Derge king, Jamyang Pema, was born in 1942 and died in 1959.

16 Michel Peissel, *Cavaliers of Kham: the Secret War in Tibet*, Willmer Brothers Limited, 1972, p. 83.

17 Tsering Shakya, *The Dragon in the Land of the Snows*, Columbia University Press, 1999, p. 141.

In the spring of 1959, Shongshong, now 17, found himself in Lhasa. How he got there, and what happened on the way, Shongshong hasn't told me. In Lhasa, the Dalai Lama, Tibet's supreme ruler (himself only 24 years old) was under increasing pressure to accede to Chinese reforms, against the wishes of his advisors, the aristocracy, and a growing proportion of the populace. For the past several months, the city had received streams of refugees from the fighting, as well as pilgrims come to celebrate the lunar New Year.

Against this background of seething, anxious crowds on Lhasa's streets, the Dalai Lama received a peculiar invitation from the Chinese army to attend a theatrical performance—without his usual retinue of bodyguards. When word of this leaked outside, people surged around the Norbulingka Gardens (where the Dalai Lama was staying at the time) to prevent him from leaving. They feared he would be kidnapped.

On the evening of the 16th of March, 1959, matters came to a head, and the decision was made to flee. In the dark of night, disguised in the clothes of a layman, the Dalai Lama left Lhasa and Tibet. During his flight to India, he was accompanied by Khampa soldiers. To this day he has not returned.

I asked Shongshong if he had ever seen the Dalai Lama, and he said yes, he had. In fact, he was part of the crowd protecting the Dalai Lama outside the Norbulingka. If he played any greater role than that, he wisely has never told me. Whatever his role was, he was subsequently arrested and spent some time in prison. Upon his release, he returned home to Derge.

Fast forward through the destructive, terror-filled insanity of the "Cultural Revolution," past the death of Mao, to the 1980s and the ascendancy of Deng Xiaoping. "When Deng Xiaoping started reforms, he reopened the monasteries," Shongshong said. "From a very young age, I had been interested in building. As a young man, I learned carpentry and clay-work. Many temples needed repairs, and people knew that I could do this, so they invited me to take charge."

In the mid-1980s the government decided to sponsor repair of the Derge Printing House, far and away the most famous and sacred site in Derge or indeed in western Sichuan. They hired Shongshong to oversee the work. During my backpacker sojourns of 1991, I had visited the Printing House and watched painters finish up the interior decorations. Shongshong had acquired considerable fame from masterminding this complex and important project.

Renovation under way at the Derge Printing House in 1991.

Shongshong had a wife and two daughters managing the family farm, in a village one day's travel from Derge. He had two sons who lived with him in a house in Derge's Old Town. The sons were both *traba*, and Shongshong was extremely proud of them. I once visited their house in Derge, expecting that the home of an expert builder like Shongshong would be a veritable palace. I was sorely disappointed, for it was as humble as the man himself: small, without decoration, and nearly empty inside.

"Things have changed a lot here," Shongshong remarked later. "You know those houses in the valley above Derge? Before, those families were very poor. Now, children can study in the village school for three years, then they can come down and attend primary school in town."

Then, to my utter amazement, he said: "These days, I think the Communist Party is doing a good job."

What is the meaning of this? I wondered. A Tibetan praising the Chinese Communist Party? Did someone tell Shongshong to say that, or was it his real opinion? The mystery added one more enigmatic layer to the old Tibetan builder, a man I would learn to work with, but would never really know.

Shongshong took me around Palpung and Pewar Monasteries, showing me what was afflicting their temples: rotten timbers, leaking roofs, crumbling clay walls, and slow but inexorable collapse. I wrote reports based on Shongshong's observations, and took hundreds of photos that I would later send to John Sanday to help him prepare for the fall expedition.

Then I took the long road back, all the way to Hong Kong, where I busied myself for a month, waiting for the time to come.

Second Mission: 1994

CHAPTER 4

IN TIBETAN Buddhist art, minute details cast a subliminal message before the eye, a seed to blossom during meditation. For example, on the right rear of Pewar's temple, forming the backdrop of one Jataka tale, is a mushrooming outcrop of *vajra-rock*. Vajra (diamond) rock is green and round on top, sharp and faceted below. Composed of many precious substances, it springs out of the earth like a flame or a flower, bursting into a wide crystalline crown. Vajra-rock has several conjoined meanings. When chanting devotion to a wrathful deity, vajra-rock arises as a reality source of the syllable *E*, which stands for *evam,* a word that opens many Buddhist scriptures and means "thus." The rock's inverted pyramid shape simultaneously represents the center of the universe and single-pointedness of mind. It is a splinter fallen from the great Mount Meru, a place beyond our physical universe, a realm of perfection and transcendence.

October 16

At last I was running a real expedition (with more than one person), and we were on the road. The monastery conservation project, Wong told me, was permanently mine now. My team consisted of John Sanday, the tenacious Razat, and a newly recruited Chinese interpreter and cook.

We had our permits safely in hand, our supplies were bought, packed, and loaded, but I was not home free—not yet. Having made a mid-afternoon start, we got only two hours down the road before the driver wanted to quit for the day. Harry the interpreter, who was a little wobbly on the driver's dialect, managed to eke out the excuse: "the generator's not producing any current."

Razat, the author, John Sanday, and Harry Wong pause for a snapshot on the way to Derge.

Harry Wong spins a prayer wheel during a stop at Lhagang.

The real reason, it gradually transpired, was that we were stopped in the man's home town, and he had decided he'd like to sleep in his own bed that night. Well, so would I—but only after the mission is done! I told him "we'll go on," and after we had stopped and gassed up and the driver had fetched some warm clothing, and after I had bought a carton of Five Pagoda cigarettes for him, we got on the road again. That was, my journal noted, the first time I ever fixed an alternator with cigarettes.

We four passengers were already great friends. During the summer permit debacle, John, Razat, and I had gone every day to the restaurant owned by Harry and his girlfriend Lily, so it seemed only natural to have Harry with us now. Harry was from a poor farming village in Guangdong province. His original given name had been Chesheng, or "Born-in-acart," because his father could not drive the family's water buffalo fast enough to reach the hospital in time. (He later changed his name to Xiaoxing, or "bright star").

No one in Harry's village had ever been to college, and Harry's parents believed that school was a place you sent children when they needed a "rest" from farming. Nevertheless, Harry excelled academically, eventually graduating with a business degree from Shenzhen College. He moved to Chengdu, met Lily (who would later have her own role to play in the project), and together they started a restaurant catering to foreigners. After a year of chatting with Western backpackers, Harry was a worldly fellow compared to most Sichuan people. He seemed more like one of us than a native of China.

John Sanday was the quintessential old Himalayan hand, having lived in Kathmandu for some decades and restored many monuments there. Tall, fiftyish, Britishly droll at times, fluent in Nepali and French as well as English, he was a born adventurer with a deep and enduring love for Himalayan peoples. He also understood buildings. John viewed each monument as a doctor might view the human anatomy: awe-inspiring when it works, and when it doesn't, a web of mind-bending puzzles. I would learn a lot from him during the coming weeks.

Razat, John's young assistant, was smart, educated, lucky to have been born into the Nepalese aristocracy, and glad for his privileges. He was a competent architect and seldom complained about anything, but it was clear that he didn't fully appreciate the adventure value of working in Kham.

Our first stop, Kangding, was a rip-roaring edge-of-the-plateau mountain metropolis, now the administrative headquarters of all Ganzi Prefecture, which takes up the eastern half of Kham.

Prior to the twentieth century, Kangding was the capital not of a Chinese prefecture called Ganzi, but a Tibetan kingdom called Chakla. It was ruled by hereditary chieftains—although their independence was tempered by militant Chinese masses just one mountain range away. Throughout recorded history, Chinese have been leaking into Chakla and

especially Kangding, an ethnic melting pot that includes other nationalities such as Yi and Hui.[18]

Dartsendo is the Tibetan name of the town. The name's meaning is
usually given as "confluence of the Dar and Tse rivers"; but there is
another, more colorful etymology. The name Darstendo sounds to Chinese ears like "Dajianlu," and this can be read to mean "Town of hurtled
arrows." According to one legend, the name arose because of a territo-
rial dispute between the local Tibetan chieftain and the nearby Chinese
ruler Zhuge Liang (A.D. 181-234). Zhuge was prime minister of the Shu[19]
state during the Three Kingdoms period. In those early days, the Tibetan
empire had not yet grown to encompass Dartsendo, which was lightly
populated by herdsmen.[20]

In the course of conducting various wars, Prime Minister Zhuge
wished to pass an army through the Ya'an district. That district, which
lies one mountain range to the east of Kangding, was then ruled by the
Dartsendo tribal chief. The two sides negotiated, with the result that the
chief agreed to withdraw his people toward the west and an arrow shot
by Zhuge would decide the new border. The crafty Zhuge sent someone
to plant an arrow on Guoda Mountain, just east of Dartsendo valley,
thereby expropriating the most possible tribal land. Afterwards, the town
became known for this treacherous incident.

Legend or not, Chinese have continued their inexorable encroach-
ment into Tibetan territory. In the first half of the twentieth century,
Kangding was a border town, with a strong Tibetan character.[21] It thrived
on trade between the two peoples, especially of Ya'an tea, which was
carried up to Kangding by Chinese coolies, then onward by yak caravans. Since 1950, however, the town's status as prefectural headquarters

18 Muslim Chinese.

19 Shu is an ancient name for Sichuan.

20 The Chinese called such people Qiang, a catch-all term for western pastoral tribes. As
Tibetan rule expanded during the period A.D. 600-900, many of these clans were subsumed
into Tibet. Since 1949 the name Qiang has designated a distinct ethnic group centered about the
town Maowen in western Sichuan. These Qiang number about 100,000 and speak a Tibeto-
Burman language.

21 From the accounts of missionaries George Patterson and Geoffrey Bull, it appears that
Kangding had roughly equal populations of Chinese and Tibetans in the 1940s.

has drawn many Han settlers, who either are posted there by the government, or migrate voluntarily to start businesses.

Despite ever-increasing numbers of Han Chinese in Kangding, some Tibetan character remains. Three of the town's original seven Tibetan monasteries survive, and its largest annual civic celebration is still Sakyamuni's birthday, marked with a week-long festival.

Kangding is the capital of Ganzi Prefecture,[22] which makes up a big chunk of Kham and is regarded by many as its cultural heart. The prefecture is considerably larger than several European countries — such as Hungary; it sprawls over 153,000 square kilometers of mountainscape, pasture, forest, and farm. The name means "white beautiful," named after a great white stone that is still found near the modern seat of Kandze County.

Ganzi Tibetan Autonomous Prefecture,[23] as it is officially named, has a special status on account of its large proportion of a "minority nationality." To be sure, the place has little if any real autonomy and is subject to the whim and wisdom of bureaucrats in Chengdu.

People in Ganzi are thinly scattered: the average is less than four per square kilometer. A 1990 census showed a total population of 627,024, of whom 75.6% were Tibetans,[24] 21.5% Han Chinese, and 2.9% belonged to other ethnic groups.[25] (The census would not have included the "floating population" of unregistered temporary residents such as soldiers, itinerate laborers, and illegal immigrants.) Han Chinese are concentrated in the towns and cities, and in the low-lying eastern county of Luding. The rest of the region is overwhelmingly Tibetan, living as farmers or herdsmen in traditional fashion. They maintain their religious traditions in 475 purportedly still-active monasteries divided among five sects.

22 In order to conveniently distinguish between Kandze county and Ganzi prefecture, I will violate the naming convention described in footnote 1 by calling them by their Tibetan and Chinese names respectively.

23 Within Sichuan Province there are two other "autonomous" prefectures: Ngawa (Aba), which is Tibetan, and Liangshan, which is inhabited by a people known as Yi.

24 Tibetans in Ganzi comprise a little more than 12% of the total Tibetans within the People's Republic of China.

25 *Annals of the Nationalities of Ganzi Tibetan Autonomous Prefecture* (Ganzi Zangzu Zizhizhou Minzu Zhi), Modern China Publishing House, 1994.

The question of who ruled Ganzi and the rest of Kham during various periods of history is contentious and complex. Two powers have vied for control: the mighty but distant Chinese emperors, and the closer but disorganized and militarily weak Lhasa government. The shifting flux of power from these two opposite poles made the kingdoms of Kham into virtual buffer states. They maintained a high degree of independence, tolerating Chinese garrisons or Lhasa tax collectors only when their demands were not excessive. The upper Yangtze River,[26] now the boundary between Sichuan Province and Tibet Autonomous Region, has often been a de facto dividing line between spheres of Tibetan and Chinese influence.

What is now Ganzi Prefecture lies on the east side of the river, and was therefore more strongly subjected to Chinese authority, waxing and waning in step with China's dynastic cycles. During periods of Chinese weakness, Ganzi's many principalities reverted to local rule, each king vying with his neighbors for land and subjects. Buddhist monasteries were key power brokers, amassing wealth and defending it with platoons of monk-soldiers when necessary. And the warring didn't stop there, recalled one exile: "Families fought against families, tribes against tribes, often for reasons that were so buried in the past that even the protagonists were not very sure what they were fighting about."[27]

Out of this endless struggle, the Derge Kingdom emerged to take a dominant position in the late seventeenth century. As I will later describe, the ruling clan governed a huge portion of Kham and amassed great wealth. Derge's regional influence is apparent today, for the dialects of surrounding territories are variants of Derge speech, which locals still say is the "most standard" in Kham.

By the mid-nineteenth century, when Derge's dominance had run its

26 In Tibetan the river is called Dri Chu, which is translated as Female Yak River by one author, although several locals I consulted were unsure if this is the true origin of the name. In Chinese, this part of the Yangtze is called Jinsha Jiang, or "river of gold sand," after its silty shores and the gold dust panned from them.

27 Jamyang Norbu, p. 32.

course, Nyarong (Xinlong) came to prominence. The Nyarong king Gonpo Namgyal conquered much of Kham, including Derge and virtually all Tibetan lands east of the Yangtze.[28] In 1865 an annoyed Lhasa government sent troops to force his submission and restore his territory to the rule of the Dalai Lama. The crafty Gonpo Namgyal decided to capitulate, making a flamboyant declaration of loyalty to the Tibetan prelate. But the ruse didn't work, for on his way home to Nyarong, the Khampa leader was murdered. One can only imagine the Khampas' fury after such treachery.

By the late nineteenth century the Manchu-led Qing Empire was reasserting authority in Ganzi; but their rule was spotty and insecure. Despite increasing warlordism and anarchy, the Qing nevertheless took umbrage when the British invaded Lhasa in 1904. Led by Sir Francis Younghusband, the British had marched from India in order to force trading rights on the reclusive Tibetans.

Fearful of deeper British infiltration into what the Chinese considered their proper sphere of influence, they began to try to subdue Tibetan lands, bringing them under the Manchu emperor in Beijing. As a first step, they sought to colonize and develop Ganzi, beginning with the territory of Bathang (Batang), which is low-lying and therefore better suited to Chinese-style agriculture. The Bathang Tibetans rebelled, compelling the Qing to take up sterner measures to bring the region under control, lest it fall into British hands.

Sterner measures arrived in the form of General Zhao Erfeng, known to Tibetans as "Butcher Zhao."[29] By 1911 he had subjugated towns and roads throughout the region now known as Ganzi, and much more besides. Chinese colonists arrived to join the soldiers already living there, and before long there were mixed marriages, resulting in half-caste children. Yet the Qing Dynasty was collapsing, and with China disintegrating into chaos, Ganzi quickly reverted to de facto local rule.

The Chinese Nationalists who replaced the Qing created a short-lived province called Xikang in 1939. Xikang consisted of present-day Ganzi

---

28 Jamyang Norbu, p. 27.

29 Eliot Sperling, "The Chinese Venture in K'am, 1904–1911, and the Role of Chao Erh-feng," *The Tibet Journal*, Vol 1, No. 2, pp. 10-36.

and some Yi and Han areas to the east. They appointed Sichuan warlord Liu Wenhui as military commander of the region. Profits from opium grown on Yi lands paid for Liu's army, which was headquartered in Ya'an, east of Ganzi.[30] Yet Liu's forces never became strong enough to wield anything more than nominal power in Ganzi. "At most the Tibetan will give only grudging obedience, even in the garrisoned towns, while the outlying districts will continue in a half-rebellious attitude yielding taxes at the point of guns from large armed forces, which they recover by ambushing and robbing."[31]

Despite *de jure* rule by Beijing's Nationalist government, three brothers called Pangdatsang established a family empire in what is now Bathang County. (Slippery politicians, the Pangdatsangs maintained close ties to the Lhasa government even while one of them, Topgay, was made a colonel in Chiang Kai-shek's army.)[32] Derge, too, was "almost autonomous" during this period.[33]

The anything-goes atmosphere that prevailed in the first half of the twentieth century encouraged foreign missionaries, who set up shop in a number of towns including Kangding, Tawu, and Bathang. Leading ragged bands of mostly Chinese converts, they doctored the sick, took in orphans, and so earned a place in the community.[34] Their legacy survives in small but indomitable congregations that have carried on to the present day despite persecution and turmoil.[35] Now, Kangding boasts both Protestant and Catholic churches in addition to its three Buddhist monasteries and a mosque serving the Hui community.

By 1935, the winds of change were in the air. Communist armies on

---

30 A. Doak Barnett, *China's Far West: Four Decades of Change,* SMC Publishing Company, Taipei, 1993, p.412.

31 Marion Duncan, *Customs and Superstitions of Tibetans,* The Mitre Press, London, 1964, p. 31.

32 John Kenneth Knaus, *Orphans of the Cold War: America and the Tibetan struggle for survival,* Public Affairs, 1998, p. 58.

33 Robert Ford, *Wind between the Worlds,* Snow Lion Graphics, p. 50.

34 André Migot, *Tibetan Marches,* Rupert Hart-Davis, 1955, p. 127. According to interviews conducted by Wong How Man in 1991 and myself in 2000, in Tawu, French Catholic missionaries were opposed by Nyimtsho Monastery, who, in 1912, burned down the Catholics' church. This came at the same time as a general exodus of Chinese from the town; some were killed by Tibetans before they could escape. The Qing government then sent in troops, who

the "Long March" arrived in Western China. Their movements were fast as lightning and just as unpredictable, utterly befuddling Chiang Kai-shek's Nationalist forces. The Communists redistributed land as they went, passed out goods taken from the storehouses of the wealthy, and picked up thousands of recruits among grateful peasants. Three contingents crossed Ganzi Prefecture at various times, by various routes. They met up in the seat of Kandze County where they successfully established the first Tibetan Soviet in 1936.[36] After camping for some months, the troops departed, marching onward to rendezvous with Mao Zedong's forces in the north.[37]

Until this time the Communists had been treating with great care the local people whose land they crossed—especially non-Han ethnic groups—scrupulously paying for every grain of rice. But by the time they reached the Tibetan plateau, battle fatigue, illness, and the threat of starvation had undermined discipline. In Amdo (northeast Tibet), many Tibetans fled their homes, so Mao's soldiers helped themselves to whatever food they could find. Tibetans repaid the Red Army by ambushing stragglers, stripping them, and leaving them to die. Red troops in Ganzi were better behaved than those in Amdo, and met milder opposition; some were even helped by locals. Mao Zedong later said that food taken from the Tibetans was "our only foreign debt."

After a long and bloody civil war, the Communists defeated Chiang Kai-shek's armies, and with the help of Allied powers evicted the Japanese. On October 1, 1949, Mao stood in Tian An Men Square and declared the birth of New China. His People's Liberation Army,

---

defeated the monastery's forces and restored order. The Chinese soldiers then took over the monastery, making it into a garrison, but it was later returned to the monks. The Catholics demanded compensation for their lost church, which led to the construction of a new church, made of brick and timber, in mixed European-Chinese style. The ruins can still be found in Tawu near the Chengguan Primary School.

35 In the case of Catholics, Kangding has a new church with about 100 members, led by the only priest in the region. Tawu has a congregation numbering about 20, evenly divided between Han and Tibetan, which meets in a small brick building in the town's suburbs. Active Catholic communities also exist in Trango and Danba.

36 Tsering Shakya, *The Dragon in the Land of the Snows*, Columbia University Press, 1999, p. 34.

37 Harrison Salisbury, *The Long March: The Untold Story*, Harper & Row, New York, 1985.

seasoned by decades of fighting, promptly set about "liberating" Tibet.

Commander Liu Wenhui quickly cut a deal with the Communists, thereby ensuring that all of Ganzi would be bloodlessly transferred to Mao's new government.[38] The People's Liberation Army then pushed roads through Ganzi so that they could use the region as a launch pad for attacks west. On the west side of the Yangtze, Tibetan troops resisted Chinese advances, but were ill-equipped, disorganized, and further hampered by the fact that some Khampas—bitterly resentful of corrupt Lhasa administrators—went over to the other side. Within a short time, key Tibetan towns and cities were under Communist rule. Maps were redrawn to eliminate Xikang Province. Ganzi was joined to Sichuan, where it remains to this day.

Ganzi, therefore, is a region of strong Tibetan traditions, yet has a history of political separation from Lhasa and Central Tibet. "They were Khampas first, and then Tibetans," writes one observer.[39] Elsewhere on the plateau, Buddhist monasteries were nearly all subsumed by the Gelug sect, but not in Ganzi or indeed most of Kham. Doctrinal diversity thrives in Ganzi, where all four of the major sects are represented—Nyingma, Sakya, Kagyu, Gelug—as well as the indigenous Bön faith. In fact, within Ganzi there are three counties (Serdar, Pelyul, Nyarong) that contain not a single Gelug monastery.

Inhabitants of Ganzi are Khampas, and are therefore distinguished from other Tibetans by their greater height, their more aquiline noses, and their distinctive forms of dress—especially the red tassel worn by men in their long, braided hair. They disdain the use of fancy honorifics common to Lhasa speech, and consider themselves straight-talking compared to "cunning" Lhasa folk. (Lhasa people, in turn, stereotype Khampas as troublemakers and barbarians.) A popular aphorism proclaims that Lhasa has the best religion, Amdo the best horses, and Kham the best men. They are proud of their reputation for toughness and ferocity in hand-to-hand fighting. "A real man does not sit in comfort, a goat

38 Barnett, p. 448.

39 Knaus, p. 70.

stays not on a level place," well describes the Khampa outlook.[40]

Conquest of Kham by the Communists has all but eliminated the internecine warring that for centuries honed Khampas' combat skills. Now, decades have passed since the days of the old kingdoms of Derge, Bathang, Trehor, Nyarong, and Chakla. Interregional conflict still occurs over grazing rights and other minor matters, and dialect still serves as a banner of origin. Nevertheless, Khampas of Ganzi are gradually forging a united identity.

40 Marion Duncan, *Customs and Superstitions of Tibetans*, The Mitre Press, London, 1964, p. 32.

CHAPTER 5

AT THE NORTH END of Pewar's east wall, Gautama Buddha's life unfolds, a fantastic melding of legend and history. The Buddha is shown first in the Tushita Heaven awaiting the precise moment of his birth. He selected as parents Suddhodana, King of the Sakyas, and Queen Mara, who was impregnated as she slept by a white elephant entering her side. Ten months later prince Siddartha Gautama was born.

The young prince learned well, and became strong. When he came of age, he married the beautiful Yasodhara, who bore him a son. Together they enjoyed pleasure and ease in the king's palace.

As time went by, the handsome Prince Siddartha became restless to break out of his golden cage. Outside the walls, he was stunned to learn that the lot of ordinary humankind was not joyful ease, but old age, sickness, and death. The horror of this inescapable suffering compelled him to reexamine his sheltered life.

The prince decided to leave the palace. He discarded horses, servants, raiment, and family to became a wandering ascetic. Through his own iron will, he forced himself to endure agonizing privations, until his emaciated body was near death. Yet still no answer to humankind's suffering was offered him. In despair, he sat beneath a fig tree and began to meditate. Days later, when he opened his eyes, he knew the answer, the Four Noble Truths: that life is inseparable from suffering; that suffering is caused by misknowing; that from this suffering there exists a means of escape; and the eight rules for living that constitute the path to freedom.

This story is told on Pewar's walls.

October 17

Reaching Kangding with my team in late autumn, I was overjoyed to be out of the swelter and smog of Chengdu, to see snow covered-mountains, inhale the sweet perfume of evergreens, and spin prayer wheels at Ngachu Gonpa right outside the guest house. For centuries Kangding was a trading center between Chinese and Tibetans; it's still a place where the cultures mingle. Kangding streets are a heterogeneous parade of Khampa traders, bureaucrats in dark suits, drivers of logging trucks, scarf-swathed Muslims, Tibetan grannies with long white braids, college students, and schoolchildren in red sweaters. John Sanday, Harry, Razat, and I stopped here for two days to change transport and to buy tools we would need for the work ahead.

By now I've traveled the Sichuan-Tibet highway to Derge so many times that memories layer on top of memories, like an oft-crooned lullaby. Each region has its own flavor, for differences in dress, architecture, and dialect are still strong. Towns are strung along the highway like multicolored beads, growing successively farther apart and more rustic as one heads west.

Beyond Kangding is a pass, Tseto La (4290 meters, 14,075 feet), that leads to the Minyag region. Minyagpa live in enormous stone houses that stand like medieval castles over the land. Minyag is relatively prosperous owing to its proximity to Kangding and "the Innerland" as people here refer to lowland China. After the little town of Dzongzhab (Xinduqiao), the road forks, cleaving into the northern and southern highways across Kham. We chose the northern route, which leads to Derge.

A few hours later the medieval Tibetan town of Lhagang (Tagong) appeared, with its enormous Sakya monastery and field of 108 stupas. We stopped to pay a visit to the gonpa. At last the sun was high and the chill air was warming—to the relief of poor Harry, a Guangdong boy appalled by the Tibetan climate. Not long after we resumed our journey, the pavement ended, and we began jouncing on rutted, packed earth.[41]

---

41 In 1998 the government began a multiyear project to lay pavement on both north and south routes all the way across western Sichuan to the TAR border.

A pass brought us to the next world, Tawu (Daofu) part of the Trehor Kingdom. Mongol scribes record that an emissary of Kubilai Khan,
passing through this region in the thirteenth century, fell in love with a
Tibetan girl and with her fathered a child. The boy was called Homa
Sangbo, which means "Mongolian boy born casually." He grew up to
found a dynasty of tribal headmen. Eight generations later, with the support of Mongol allies, his descendent Onglo expanded the clan's territory
to include present-day Tawu and the next two counties west. Onglo's
five children established the five Trehor states: Beri, Kangsar, Mazur,
Trewo, and Trango. They forcibly converted existing monasteries to
Gelug, and caused many new Gelug monasteries to be built.

Echoes of the region's Mongol past can still be heard in the Tawu
dialect, which is markedly different from other regional languages. Their
architecture, however, is marvelously Tibetan and renowned on the eastern plateau. Tawu houses look like chocolate cake, with their white-
washed walls and timbers painted cocoa brown. The trim is so white
that the houses appear perpetually snow-covered.

Trehor continues to the next county, Trango (Luhuo), where a mag-
nitude 7.9 earthquake in 1973 shook the beautiful houses apart. Trango
is therefore a new-looking town, large (it has five streets), overlooked by
a sprawling campus of a monastery up on a hill. From Trango our van
ground up to Latseka Pass (3,962 meters, 12,999 feet). Then we rumbled
three hours to the next town, Kandze.

Kandze County,[42] also of Trehor, is a spectacular place. Its heart is the
wide, rich Yi Chu valley, one of the few east-west corridors in the region
and therefore a major trade route from time immemorial. On the valley's
south side is an immense blade-like range, perpetually snow covered. To
the north, velveteen pasture coats swelling hills, which are seamed by
mountain-borne streams. The valley floor is blanketed with barley fields
and dotted with sturdy farmhouses of timber and adobe.

At the center of it all is the Kandze county seat. It's a dusty, rough-and-
tumble, Wild West kind of town, puddled over a broad plain along the
Yalong River. We checked into the county guest house, which was the

42 Not to be confused with its namesake Ganzi Prefecture, a much larger entity.

only place where foreigners could legally stay. It was hardly luxurious: four beds and a table in each room, outhouse across the yard, spittoons in the hallway, drifting cigarette smoke. Hoping for uninterrupted rest, I bought all the beds in one room; but to no avail. Echoing shouts in the hallway, drivers hawking their perennially phlegmy throats, and engines gunning in the yard kept me awake half the night

Morning was snapping cold and acutely clear. We cruised out at dawn, zooming past shimmering gold farmland, raising an enormous plume of dust in our wake. Every few kilometers brought another monastery; Gelugpas have several large ones here and so dominate the county.

After Kandze, humanity thins out. The land spreads and rises, leaving farmers below to their scrabbling labors. Above 4000 meters (13,123 feet), there are only yaks, nomads, and pasture. During my previous trip, the herdsmen at been at high summer camps, invisible from the highway. But now they were close by and waved at our van as we passed.

We climbed to a pass, then dropped to Manigango, a fragile knot of humanity caught like a cobweb on a fork in the road. At 3800 meters above sea level, Manigango demands fortitude; it is frequented by Tibetan nomads but Chinese settlers are few. It's places like this where the traveler will find the most swashbuckling, horse-riding, dagger-wielding Khampas. If you're looking for red-tasseled men in broad felt hats, red-cheeked turquoise-bedecked women, caparisoned horses, yak caravans, feral dogs, dust devils, white-hot sun, and sudden thunderstorms, this is where to come. Or better yet, leave the highway, hire a horse, and follow the nomads to higher pastures still.

Our driver took us to the Chinese hangout, a depot on the eastern end of town, where we had a lunch of stir-fry and rice. Then we pushed on. Slowly, we climbed to Tro La, at 4916 meters (16,129 feet) the last major hurdle on the path to Derge. Mountains pinched our valley, lifting us higher and higher, until abruptly the road jumped away, zigzagging heavenward on a path pencilled onto granite scrag. It's mind-boggling to imagine the heroic tenacity—and desperation—of the wretches who built this highway, here dynamiting a path out of solid rock, there stacking boulders, elsewhere quarrying blocks by hand. Even the heavy stone retaining walls are not absolute protection from avalanche from above, or from a landslide that collapses the road beneath you. The highway is so narrow that in winter authorities allow only one-way traffic: eastbound in the morning, westbound after 2 p.m. Nevertheless, every year has its fatalities, especially when snow falls thickly and truck tires, even those wearing chains, can skid sideways without warning.

The top of Tro La is decorated with a Chinese pagoda wrapped in prayer flags, rocks piled by triumphant travelers, and a confetti of paper *lungta* hurled into the wind with a cry of "O lha so o!" After the obligatory photograph, we descended painstakingly, lest some mishap catapult us from the mountain. Gradually we dropped through mist to a place where the road could uncoil and stretch itself along a streamlet called Zi Chu. Strengthened by a hundred icy trickles from the Tro La Range, this river would lead us west.

The Zi Chu valley is the heart of the Derge Kingdom.[43] Unlike the grandiose spaces of Kandze, Derge is smaller, warmer, and greener; Tolkien might have imagined such a valley when he planted his Hobbits in a place called The Shire. Rock faces enclose the river, plunging it into shadow. The cliffs open periodically to display enchanting log houses set among curving fields.

The rulers of this wonderland trace their family back more than fifty generations. According to *Genealogy of the Derge Kings*, the Derge clan began in the sixth century with a warrior called Langchajia. A murky character, he is not counted as the first of the line, but rather his great grandson, Gar Tongtsen Yulzung, prime minister to Songtsen Gampo (617-650), the first great Tibetan king. Gar Tongtsen was extremely powerful in the Lhasa court; after the king's death he became regent to the heir, a grandson. Gar Tongtsen died in 667, leaving four sons: two became prime ministers, and two were military commanders who spearheaded the building of the Tibetan empire.[44]

By the late seventh century the Tibetan king was growing distrustful of the Gar family's power. According to one source, all four brothers

---

43 Derge County actually begins at a pass east of Manigango (see map on page xi). Modern-day Derge is considerably reduced from its former extent, which included Pelyul (Baiyu) County, Sershul (Shiqu) County, Jomda (Jiangda) County, and Dengko (Dengke).

44 Tsepon W.D. Shakyapa, *Tibet: A Political History*, Potala Publications, 1984, p. 29.

died, three of them of unnatural causes connected to the family's fall from grace. The *Annals of Derge County*, however, have it that two (other?) sons were Bön monks, and the younger of these escaped to Kham with remaining family members in 699.

In Kham, the family prospered. Six centuries later, when the clan reached its 30th generation, a younger brother won favor in the Mongol Court, who were then patrons of Tibetan Buddhism and rulers of China. The brother was enfeoffed by the Mongols with a large territory centered on Pelyul. He was awarded the title "Master of Ten Benevolences of the Four Orders" (*De zhi ge chu*),[45] which was later shortened to Derge ("virtuous community" or "land of benevolence") and adopted as the clan's name.

In the early fifteenth century, under the protection of Ling Pönbo, (King of Ling), the Derge family moved to Changra (Gongya) in the Zi Chu valley. There they settled as prominent citizens.

The 36th Derge clan chief, Botar Tashi Sengge, is described in the *Annals* as a brave and resourceful general under Ling Pönbo. The Pönbo admired his general's pretty daughter, Dzedan, and desired to take her as concubine. The Derge family demanded as brideprice as much land as a yak could plow in one day. Ling Pönbo agreed, so Tashi Sengge ordered his servants to start plowing from Korlondo (Keluotong) on the Zi Chu River and work downstream. By dawn of the next day, they had covered a 30-kilometer-long strip of prime farmland. In this way the Derge clan acquired the rich and fertile territory that would be their future empire's heart.

The family's fortunes reached an apex when King Denba Tsering (1678-1739) came to power. He initiated a period of aggressive expansion that pushed back the Trehors to the east and brought huge portions of Kham into his domain. According to the *Annals*, he "subdued thirty-seven tribes in Sershul, conquered five tribes in the pastoral areas of Jomda and Konjo in the present-day Tibet Autonomous Region (TAR), eliminated the remaining local chieftains in Derge and Pelyul, and defeated a plot hatched by the Konjo chieftain and a Mongolian chieftain

45 Yang Jiaming, *Dege Sutra-Printing Academy*, Sichuan People's Publishing House, 2000, p. 48.

in Qinghai to attack him from both sides." A devout Buddhist, Denba Tsering ran his government from within Gönchen Monastery. He used some of his immense wealth to found the Derge Printing House in 1729, and built a string of monasteries, including Palpung.

After four long, dusty days on the road, we made our triumphant entry into Derge. Shongshong and Tenzeng Nyima, the young abbot of Pewar Monastery, hailed us from the street as we drove past noodle shops near the bus station. Having received my telegram, they were expecting us. I shouted to the driver to stop. Alighting even before the van was halted, I ran to my two dear friends and we exchanged hearty, heartfelt hand-holds.

That night, at a summit in Pewar Rinpoche's living room, I was inducted into program leadership. What precipitated the lesson was Shongshong's request for 15,000 yuan to buy a tractor for Pewar. I promptly unzipped my money belt, and started counting out the cash. Then I thought: wait a moment.

"Why do you want to buy a tractor?"

Harry translated my question, and the answer came back: "To carry wood to rebuild the monastery." Shongshong explained that the forest next to the monastery could not be cut—it was protected by law. They would have to go a kilometer away to get fresh timber for building.

"But there's no road yet. Why do you want to buy the tractor now?"

The answer that came back to this one was jumbled. I pressed for further information from Shongshong, who was all for starting construction at Pewar right away. How can he start building when there's no wood at the site yet? What are they going to do with this tractor after the project is over when all they've got is an isolated one-kilometer road to drive it on? How did people move timber in the days before tractors were invented, anyway?

Lacking the language skills to really nail down all these fine points of reasoning, I had decided just to trust Shongshong and Tenzeng Nyima to do the right thing, but Harry, who had been to business school back in Guangdong, warned: "Tibetan people are like peasants; they don't understand about planning and they don't understand budgets."

John Sanday offered, "You need to set up an accounting system. I've done the same thing for my work team at Angkor, so I can help you do it here." He launched into an outline of semiannual inspections, accountants wielding tidy columnar notebooks, Khmer foremen collecting signatures on preprinted receipts from Khmer workers, monthly reports. It all seemed a bit fabulous and improbable for Kham.

Meeting with Shongshong, Harry Wong, and John Sanday.

"Think of this project as a business," advised Harry. "You're the boss. You can't *ask* them what to do, you have to *tell* them."

"And I thought I was hiring a cook!" All this from a skinny Cantonese born in a farming village several million light-years from here. Sure, he had bootstrapped his life out of dismal poverty, clawed his way to a higher education, opened a restaurant in Chengdu, and made a success of it. But he sure didn't know Tibet. All the way here he had been complaining of a sick stomach and an altitude-induced headache. He had never seen snow before in his life. When we arrived in Derge, his first comment—very Cantonese—was: "God, there are so many dogs here. Wouldn't it be nice to eat them?"

Throughout the next day, as we were setting up bank accounts, Harry and John kept telling me how to manage project money and "handle" the Tibetans. I wondered, why are they telling *me* about all of this? Why can't they just implement their ideas without lecturing me? Then I remembered: they think *I'm* the leader. Gulp. And so I listened and tried to learn.

John and Harry helped me structure the accounting system so that Shongshong couldn't run off and buy an unauthorized tractor with our money. We kept telling him we wanted to delay that purchase, but he couldn't seem to get it into his head. Harry, the Special Economic Zone sophisticate, complained about how illogical these "Chinese" can be in cooperative ventures with foreigners, how you tell them one thing and they solemnly agree and then run off and do another. It seemed to me that Harry was right, but I wished I could get back the respect I had for Shongshong before, when he was my admired teacher guiding me across Derge's magical mountains.

In due course—which means much later than we would have liked—the expedition set off for Pewar and Palpung. To my annoyance, we were assigned an escort: officer Malu of Public Security. He was sent by the county government to "ensure our safety" and, more important, to make sure we refrained from anything political. A open-bed truck appeared to carry us out of town to the trailhead. John Sanday, Razat, and I volunteered to ride in the truck bed with the baggage, leaving Harry and the cop to nab choice places in the cab.

It's rule in these parts that a ride going anywhere always attracts extra passengers who somehow attach themselves. Prior to launch, John panned his video camera across Shongshong, Tenzeng Nyima, and the unwashed, uninvited, unexplained Khampas who were with us in back of the truck. As John filmed, he narrated in BBC deadpan: "And here are our fellow passengers as we begin the trip to Pewar" (zooming in on their whisky bottle), "and here are the refreshments."

When we arrived at the trailhead, we found that the horses and guides were not there—they had come yesterday while we were unexpectedly tied up in meetings. A messenger was dispatched to summon them. Hours later (with Razat asking every thirty minutes "when will the horses come?"), they arrived, a train of jingling animals done up in saddles and colorful blankets, a most pleasing sight. Our gear and ourselves were divvied up and mounted. We had gotten hardly 100 meters down the road before Harry was thrown from his horse. He lay in the dust, silent and wincing, until we picked him up. Then, to his credit, he got right back on, plugged in his Walkman headphones, and rode regally with us into the mountains.

Caravan is assembled
for the trip to Pewar.

The trail to Pewar (where I had decided we would go first) starts on the eastern shore of the Dri Chu River, better known to the outside world as the upper Yangtze. This flowing colossus is one of several gargantuan north-south rivers carving deep corrugations into the highlands of Kham. It separates Derge and the rest of Ganzi Prefecture from Tibet Autonomous Region, and it was a major reason why Lhasa's power had such difficulty penetrating east.

Now we were leaving that muddy, swirling torrent behind us, marching into the mountains of western Sichuan. We followed a plunging tributary called the Bei Chu, whose icy waters tumble down from the snowy peaks and perennial glaciers of the Tro La Range. Our trail was a narrow one, and unpopulated. It climbed high and low along the riverbanks, alternately slipping into forest or tracing along high cliff walls. The trail had recently been improved; in 1991, it had been impassable to pack animals, and therefore little used. Even Shongshong, prior to my previous visit, had never traveled this way and had never visited Pewar Monastery before.

Villagers who provided transportation for the team.

In good conditions, the journey should have needed about four hours of riding. We started late, however, and soon it was dusk. As the light faded, those of us who had been walking were persuaded by the wranglers to mount, for after sunset, equine eyes are better than human. I was thinking of Robert Frost's lines, "Whose woods these are I think I know/His house is in the village though" when John's mount's front legs buckled on some treacherous boulders, dumping the gallant architect head over heels to the ground. Fortunately, neither man nor beast was hurt. "There were moments when I was shit-scared," John said later.

As our surroundings faded to black, the policeman Malu suddenly seemed not nearly so unnecessary as I had thought. He took my horse's lead and tied it to his saddle, guiding us along the now-invisible track.

I later learned that Malu had been born on the grasslands, to nomad parents. He didn't know his birthday, for his mother and father hadn't thought to write it down. When he was seventeen he joined the army, where he learned to read and write Chinese but not Tibetan, a deficiency that embarrassed him forever after. Upon discharge from the army, he was offered a police job. Thanks to his work in the foreign affairs office, he had many incarnate friends abroad whom he had escorted around Derge over the years; on his wrist he wore a treasured watch given him by Situ Rinpoche. Malu was a widower, his wife having died a few years after their daughter was born. He lived a lonely bachelor life in a Tibetan house on the east side of town.

It was cold sitting on top of that pony. About the time I thought my hands and feet were turning into icicles, we crossed the barley fields that I knew meant Pewar was near. As we went over a wooden bridge and up a steep slope, our long caravan bunched. Out of the black, I saw the lead man's flashlight playing on an ochre-colored wall. A hand grabbed my horse's lead and guided him through an opening that I knew must be the monastery gate.

Now the darkness was broken by several flashlight beams, and candles illuminated the paper of a few windows upstairs. The young abbot Tenzeng Nyima had ridden ahead to announce us, so a dozen hands were ready to help us off our horses and unload our goods. Upstairs, my old friend the old concierge monk Tsetra was waiting for us, pitcher of butter-tea in hand. Candlelit tables were spread with meat, dough fritters, hard candy, and a great bowl of tsampa[46] topped with a lug of butter. Harry took one look at all this, then dived into our baggage to dig out some freeze-dried stroganoff, which he began preparing for himself, John, and Razat. I was too famished to wait; I sat down before the Tibetan spread and hungrily fell to.

---

46 Tsampa is made by first parching barley kernels, then grinding them into flour. The flour is then mixed with tea, butter, and sometimes sugar to make edible dough that needs no further cooking. This is the staple food of Tibet.

⤳ ॐ

CHAPTER 6

AT THE CENTER-bottom of Pewar's west wall is painted an elephant barreling at full speed. He is passing beneath a tree, and his hapless rider grasps at a branch to try to save himself. Behind is a white-robed figure urging the elephant on.

The story is probably Nalagiri the Elephant, a jataka tale about a plot concocted by Buddha's evil cousin, Devadatta, to bring about The Perfected One's demise. In his unbridled quest for power, Devadatta tried poison, he tried assassins, and he sent seductresses, but nothing worked. Then he hit upon the notion of sending an enraged beast to accomplish his evil intent. Devadatta stole to the royal stables, where he poured wine into the trough of Nalagiri the Elephant. After the animal was quite drunk, Devadatta's hirelings tormented him with jabbing spears and a clamor of cymbals and drums. Enraged, Nalagiri broke free from his chains. He thundered into the street, wrecking destruction with every step.

The Buddha, however, was unafraid. He stepped toward Nalagiri, offering tender, compassionate words. The elephant's madness was quelled; he knelt before the Buddha, utterly tamed. All the populace rejoiced at the miracle, and the evil Devadatta slunk away.

October 25

⤳ ॐ

In the morning, John Sanday and Razat began the work of inspecting Pewar Monastery's main temple. Tibetan monasteries normally consist of many buildings, but Pewar is small. It possesses a single temple fronted by a U-shaped two-story building that creates a courtyard, a typical arrangement. Beyond that and a few houses belonging to monks, Pewar had no other structures. The temple building was where we would live and work.

Pewar's main temple had been constructed in about the year 1735—quite recent by the standards of Asia. It was called, accordingly, *lhaser*, or "new temple."[47] There had been a much older temple dating back to the founding of the monastery more than 700 years ago, but now there was little sign of it. Above and south of the *lhaser* was a village of about a dozen houses, some of which were inhabited by monks.

Normally, Tibetan monasteries are either placed on a high prominence, or else sited on a south-facing slope; but Pewar is unusual for being located on the valley floor. Nevertheless, the setting is stunning. Mountainsides rise steeply on all sides, some covered thickly in old-growth Yunnan fir, some stair-stepping upwards in dramatic terraces, still others showing only stark, naked crag. Above the monastery, on the summit of Bomo Pundzang hill, lies some fairly well-preserved ruins. This three-story palace was said to belong to General Nyesa Aden, who fought in the service of King Gesar, a mythic Tibetan warrior born north of here.

Below the monastery flows the frothing torrent of the Bei Chu. The two shores are joined by a charming cantilever log bridge, offering passage to Pewar folks wishing to cross over to Ben-nye Mountain on the far side. The Bei Chu is enlarged by a muscular, spreading tributary called Gulung Chu, over which farmers have erected a water-powered mill. Facing Pewar across the Gulung Chu are scallops of terraced farmland running ribbon-like up the mountain. Footpaths meander about the neighborhood in every direction, some of them caravan trails to more distant parts.

Pewar was established more than 700 years ago by two men: a brother and a disciple of Kyupa Jigten Gonpo (1143–1217). The disciple, Palden

47 Much of the historical background on Pewar and Palpung that I will present here was collected by Wong How Man, and is published in the 1992 report "Buddhist Monasteries of Ganzi Tibetan Autonomous Prefecture, Western Sichuan, China," available from the Kham Aid Foundation.

Pewar Monastery and its mountain setting.

Shangchub Lingpa, was a lama of some importance, for he founded the Drigung subsect of the Kagyu lineage. It is said that he was one of thirteen disciples permitted to travel under a decorated canopy—a symbol of exalted status in Tibet. In its early days, therefore, Pewar belonged to the Kagyu order, and it came under the jurisdiction of the Beri king in Kandze, ruler of territory to the east of Derge. In 1639, the Beri king was defeated by the Mongol armies of Gushri Khan, leaving Pewar to be grabbed by Derge. The Derge king converted Pewar to the Sakya order, which it has remained ever since.

Pewar's "new temple" was the last of several building projects undertaken by the great king Denba Tsering, so all the gold he had left in his construction budget was allotted to it. Pewar was, therefore, exceedingly well furnished. Before 1950, the temple had more than 100 gold statues and a famous 1.5-meter-high gold statue of Sakyamuni that was said to have opened its mouth and spoken. The monastery also possessed the only Lithang edition of the Kangyur (commentaries on Sakyamuni's commandments) remaining on the entire Tibetan plateau. All of these treasures were stolen or destroyed during the Cultural Revolution.

Thank goodness Pewar did not lose its murals! On the ground floor of the main temple there are 28 panels: more than 300 square meters of sacred deities, images from stories, and intricate decorations, many of them highlighted in gold that was miraculously untouched. Upstairs, in the lantern of the temple, are six more panels, adding a further 43 square meters of artistic treasure. (An additional three upstairs panels were poorly executed modern replacements for paintings already lost.)

With so many temples in the region either destroyed by political upheaval or unadvisedly "repaired" by well-meaning abbots, the paintings at Pewar now represent the finest surviving set of Buddhist murals in western Sichuan. They, and not the building itself, were the reason we were trying to repair Pewar.

Actually "repair" is a misnomer; we were "conserving" Pewar. As John Sanday frequently reminded me: "If you can find a way to keep as much of the original timber as possible, you save money and you save history." His job was to do this while reversing decades of neglect. We also hoped to solve some problems common to Tibetan buildings, such as poor ventilation of cooking fires, earthquake instability, and leaky roofs.

Steadfastly ignoring the clear blue sky, warm autumn sun, and beckoning mountain vistas, John and Razat prowled Pewar's roof, their faces turned downward. Its complicated two-tiered design of layered mud and wood seemed at first inscrutable, but John didn't need long to diagnose Pewar's trouble: "The problem with these buildings is that they're always overladen. They put too much clay on to stop the water going through."

Pewar's main temple, like virtually all Tibetan buildings, was of post-and-beam construction, meaning that most of the roof's weight was carried by timber. The roof was clay, which needs constant maintenance to remain rainproof, so as to protect interior timber from damp and rot. "Since 1969 no one has taken care of this monastery," said Shongshong, wrapping on a column with his knuckles to show John the hollow sound that came from inside. "The main problem is water."

Indeed it was. Above the columns, capitals were warped and discolored by damp. Above the capitals were thick square beams, and more logs placed crosswise, all stained and sagging. The '93 earthquake had yanked some crossbeams several centimeters out of the clay wall, pulling up bits of mural that tumbled to the floor, two stories below. On top of the rotting understructure rested unimaginable tons of a double-decker roof composed of layered timber, packed clay, and a rim of overhanging flagstones.

The more I looked at Pewar's main temple, the scarier it seemed. One more earthquake would surely bring it down, burying murals, treasures, and people in the process. No wonder Shongshong was in such a hurry to get started. Even if no tremblers came, the upper murals were doomed, for the flimsy wattle-and-daub walls they were painted on were slowly collapsing. It would take extraordinary measures to save the upper murals, and if the roof was not fixed soon then even the lower murals would be lost.

Our plan of action was immediately clear. John Sanday explained, "Most important is to reduce the roof's weight. Then we put in a polythene sheet to stop the water going through. We'll have to remove the paintings, repair the roof, then reaffix the paintings. This is a specialist job."

Of course we didn't have a mural specialist handy, but John had recommendations on whom I could hire for the next mission. There was plenty to do in the meantime. Razat got busy drawing cross-sections and digging holes in the roof to discover how thick the clay really was and what lay underneath.

The murals in the lower hall were, luckily, painted on the inside surface of rammed-earth walls that were largely undamaged. These paintings were protected from leaks and could safely remain in place while the building was repaired. Despite age and dirt, the craftsmanship of the lower murals was still striking—magnificent. But I had work to do, and little time to spend studying these amazing works.

In centuries past, Derge's profusion of monasteries created a demand for thankas and wall paintings; moreover, the feudal elite were eager buyers of commissioned works of art. A thanka is a traditional Tibetan-style scroll painting made on canvas that is then sewn into a frame of silk brocade and hung on the wall. They are commissioned for many purposes: as guides for reflection and meditation, to ensure good health and prosperity, to assist a recently deceased family member into a better rebirth, as a religious offering or reference tool. The subject varies accordingly: peaceful, wrathful, or protective deities; Buddhas and Bodhisattvas, great teachers, mandalas, the Wheel of Life, medical and astrological charts. Mural paintings—in contrast to thankas—are made in generally the same styles, with a similar range of subjects, but their purpose is more decorative, and their benefits confer upon the monastery at large and not on any individual.

Unlike Western artists, Tibetan painters strove not to innovate, but to master and develop their technique within existing prescribed forms. Artists were expected to conform precisely to proportions set down by past masters for each traditional subject. (Even today, art students rely on published manuals to tell them how to paint.) Any artist daring to experiment with proportion or composition could expect scathing criticism from peers and teachers. In keeping with this ideal of selfless devotion to divine precedent, Tibetan painters rarely sign or date their works.

Tibetan sacred painting came from Indic Buddhist traditions, following on the heels of Buddhism itself, brought to Tibet during the reign of king Songtsen Gampo in the mid-seventh century. By that time, Buddhism had already taken root in Nepal, Kashmir, Pakistan, Afghanistan, Khotan, and China. Each of these regions was nurturing its own artistic traditions, so there were rich opportunities for cross-fertilization. In Tibet, Indo-Nepali schools dominated, imported from the Kathmandu valley by traveling Newar painters. It was not until the fifteenth century that a truly indigenous Tibetan style of painting appeared. Known as the Man-bris school,[48] it employed novel pigments and incorporated some Chinese perspective techniques.

After the Man-bris school took hold there was a lull in innovation until the late sixteenth century, when the Karma Gadris, or "encamp-

---

48 Man-bris is a spelling commonly employed by art scholars. It is pronounced *Menri*.

ment style," appeared: spacious and transparent, with dominant blue-green shades.[49] Gadris's inventor is said to have been a sixteenth-century artist called Namkha Tashi. This painting tradition was patronized by the great Karma Kagyu patriarchs, who lived in tent cities moving from place to place—hence the name.

While the Gadris school was developing, Man-bris painters cleaved into old and new schools. New Man-bris, or Mansar, became very popular in Kham and came to be called the "Kham style," although it did not completely displace other traditions, all of which had adherents in Derge. In the Derge Printing House, for example, half the wood blocks for making xylographic prints are in Old Man-bris style and half in the New.[50] Yet a short distance away, murals at Palpung were made in classic Karma Gadris fashion. Indeed, during the eighteenth and nineteenth centuries, Derge and the surrounding region produced dozens of renowned painters and a great diversity of art.

Experts I have consulted about Pewar Monastery's murals disagree on the style: one said it belonged to the Old Man-bris school; another said it is Mansar or "Kham" style.[51] Determination of the style rests upon study of fine details such as the degree of rounding of mountains, the shape of the clouds, and the amount of detail packed into the backgrounds. The main figures also show subtle differences, depending on the style. In Kham, some painters mingled traditions; for example, Purbu Tsering, a great nineteenth-century Chamdo artist, showed both Old and New Man-bris influence in his work.

Since the construction of Pewar, Palpung, and the Derge Printing House, art in Kham has continued to evolve. Thangla Tsewang (1902-1985) stands preeminent in the twentieth century. He was born in the rural farming district of Athri, a day's ride from Palpung. As a boy he traveled from place to place, studying with various masters. In 1926, Thangla Tsewang worked on Palpung's Gadris-style murals, which brought him fame as a "magically emanated artist." He did not stick

---

49 The S in Gadris is not pronounced.

50 Kunchok Tenzin, personal communication.

51 See Appendix II.

exclusively to Gadris; he also created Old Man-bris figures that were carved into printing blocks at the Derge Printing House, and he experimented with Chinese and even foreign methods of representation. He later went to central Tibet to serve as the 16th Karmapa's secretary. During the Cultural Revolution, he rescued many monastic treasures from the ravages of the Red Guards. After revival of Buddhist practice in Derge, he oversaw reconstruction of Palpung's main chanting hall and trained many young painters.

Although the Derge Printing House is not primarily an institution for training painters, it has influenced the development of art as the region's most important cultural landmark. Its wood block collection holds some 100 xylographic figures showing proper design and proportions for many classic subjects. Prints from these large blocks are inexpensive to make and were transported to distant sites where they served as models.

The Derge Printing House is rated as a national cultural treasure by the Chinese government and is therefore protected by law.[52] To Tibetans, the institution is sacred and priceless. During daylight hours, endless streams of people can be seen walking on the circular path around the building, a practice thought to bring benefit to all sentient beings.

Pewar, Palpung, and the Derge Printing House share a great deal of history. The foundation of the Printing House was laid in 1729 upon the orders of King Denba Tsering. The building took twenty-one years to complete.[53] Carving of the printing plates was accomplished very slowly, as subsequent kings commissioned various works one by one. They sent scholars to wander the plateau in search of documents to serve as reference to Derge's teams of carvers. Day after day, month after month, the carvers sat incising Tibetan and Sanskrit sentences into specially prepared blocks of red birch in a process that is still used today. Thus, over the course of 250 years, the library was built up.

---

52 The special status of the Printing House would have made it difficult to get permission for foreigners to work on it. Subsequently, conservators that I brought to Derge did examine the paintings and declared them urgently in need of conservation.

53 Karma Gyaltsen, "Introduction to the Derge Printing House," article in Chinese published in an unknown volume.

After the Communist Party took control of China, the Printing House was converted into a hospital, and all printing ceased. During the 1966–76 Cultural Revolution, bands of fanatical young Maoists roved over China destroying everything that represented the old social order,

Craftsmen carving blocks for the Derge Printing House.

especially its scholarship. But Zhou Enlai intervened on behalf of the Printing House, commanding that it be spared. Printing blocks, some dating back to the 1600s, were hidden by monks. One story has it that some monks passed themselves off as doctors so they could protect precious materials still in the building.

In 1979, printing was allowed to resume, although the building was in sad shape because it had not been maintained for many years. In the mid-1980s, the government allocated funds for repair of what they regarded as an important cultural site. They hired Shongshong to oversee the work, which he did most assiduously. Repairs were completed in 1991, and now the press is back in operation, cranking out thousands of traditional loose-leaf volumes annually. Their library of 270,000 wood blocks is said to encompass 70% of classical Tibetan literary culture, including the commandments of Sakyamuni (Kangyur), commentaries

(Tengyur), writings for Bön and all four Buddhist sects. They also publish works on medicine, poetry, grammar, history, astronomy, and art.

Since the end of the Cultural Revolution, Derge's ancient greatness was slowly returning. Thanks to government support and Shongshong's skill, the Printing House was flourishing. John Sanday thought it was definitely possible to rescue Pewar Monastery's paintings. There remained one more great cultural treasure in Derge: the awesome architectural masterpiece of Palpung Monastery. That would be our next stop, and the greatest challenge of all.

CHAPTER 7

AT THE REAR of Pewar's temple is a chamber containing a painting of an opulent offering scene: two brocade-clad parents, their young child, and nine monks in attendance. They are surrounded by a multitude of gold-embellished symbols. One of these is a Wheel of the Law.

The wheel, or chakra, is an omnipresent Buddhist symbol, for life is cyclic. The Wheel of the Law has eight spokes, each one a facet of the eightfold path to liberation:

Right understanding.

Right thought.

Right speech.

Right action.

Right livelihood.

Right effort.

Right mindfulness.

Right concentration.

As the Wheel of Law turns, so causality connects our past acts to our present condition through the inescapable workings of karma. Yet we are not imprisoned by the past, for the present always offers choices. If we choose a path of compassion, then wavelets of positive karma thus generated will direct us inexorably toward wisdom. This is the message implicit in a tiny golden segment of Pewar's art.

October 28

The first sight of Palpung brought a gasp from John, Razat, and Harry—and me, too; no matter that I had been here twice before. Some 200 meters over our heads, planted on a lookout, Palpung's walls loomed gargantuan, steep, and impregnable. The main temple was like a boxcar that had slid down the mountain and come to rest just on the verge of

Left: Dilapidated condition of Palpung in 1991. Most of what's shown here collapsed during an earthquake in 1993.

Right: John Sanday inspecting a crack in Palpung's exterior wall.

flying off a ski jump. Peripheral buildings, ridiculously small by comparison, were scattered around the main temple. A rabble of Derge-style log houses ran behind the monastery, on the saddle that connected it to sacred Wuchi Mountain. Water for the community came from a thin trickle flowing down a crease in the mountain, whose pasture-covered slopes rolled upward and out of sight.

From Pewar, it had taken just over three hours to get here, but the hardest part was yet to come: a steep, dusty, backbreaking climb from the valley floor. We rode past the log houses containing the township head-quarters, which were lined up facing the Bei Chu. Then we turned our backs to the river and faced a steep path that snaked upward—up and up and up, to Palpung as it loomed on its eagle's perch.

In a photograph, Palpung's main temple looks smaller than it really is, for the eye wants to believe that its lowest row of windows belong to the first floor. But no, these are *second-floor* windows, and that makes the building twice as large as it appears at first glance. All my reports and photographs had been for naught: John Sanday was little prepared for the immensity that confronted him. "This is a mammoth, mammoth task," he would say later. "At the moment, all we're doing is irritating the ele-phant—a little gnat scratching at its side."

Walking around Palpung was like exploring a medieval castle. The ceilings were high, the rooms great, but all were sunk into musty gloom. Black soot covered beamed ceilings and obscured antique frescoes. There were so few inhabitants that we seldom saw anyone except our direct hosts. The three men and I stayed in the long-abandoned quarters of Khyentse Rinpoche, who had fled into exile in 1959. I stored my gear in a dusty, butter-blackened cabinet that once housed sacred texts. Most rooms were either empty or littered with refuse. Windows, already small and admitting little light through their paper-covered wooden lattices, were boarded up. The monastery was a maze of dark, dungeon-like chambers—most of which were too dark and uncomfortable even for rats to infest.

Like Pewar, Palpung suffered from a leaking roof that had rotted inte-rior load-bearing timbers. The wood looked fine on the outside, but when I touched the inside of a fallen split log, it crumbled like stale bread in my hand. Palpung's exterior rammed-earth walls, despite being more than a meter thick at the base, had huge cracks. Although its structural ills resembled Pewar's, what was different was the immense size of the place and how each movement propagated through the structure like a house of cards. The building was slowly bending to the force of gravity, settling like snow to match the rounded contours of the hill beneath.

To start off our inspection tour, Shongshong led us down into the basement, a maze of empty rooms and uneven dirt floors broken by protruding bedrock. Once upon a time, this was a storage area and stables. We looked at the immense outer walls and saw how cracks had penetrated all the way through. In the basement chambers was a forest of timber columns that Shongshong had inserted to stop the building from sagging. "Here it sank 20 centimeters, here it sank 10 centimeters, here it sank 40," he explained, pointing to various places on the ceiling as he showed us around.

Back in Chengdu, John Sanday had scoffed at Shongshong's request that I purchase two 25-ton jacks and haul them out here. But now, seeing the thunderously heavy weight that rested on rotting columns, John was a believer. As our inspection party worked its way upward, John and Razat brainstormed about what to do. Razat asked, "Is there any way on the ground floor we can tie things together?"

"Exactly what I was thinking," John replied. "My gut feeling is that you need to do an enormous amount of research and analyze the movement throughout the whole structure, to see if there is a pattern. This is going to take an enormous amount of time."

In the days that followed, the two architects set to work like master detectives to figure out why the building was sinking, and why the walls and floors didn't meet at right angles anymore. They measured angles, pulled up floorboards, and excavated clay. At another, less important building, John conducted an experiment in crack-repair by putting an invisible steel "stitch" in the wall.[54] Gradually, he pieced together a theory of why some parts of the building were going south, others west, and still others straight down.

The monastery's problems were more than structural, however; it had a serious morale problem, just as Situ Rinpoche had told us. The place just stank of giving up. Litter left in the courtyard was still there, unswept, days later. Despite Situ Rinpoche's letter of introduction, the monks gave us a halfhearted welcome. The villagers who were helping

---

54 First, a five-foot-long trench was excavated from the side of the building. A rebar was bent into a box shape and inserted into the hole, which was then filled with a mixture of clay and cement. The result was a repair job that didn't detract from the traditional appearance of the building.

John with his experiments were disinterested. "They just don't care," he complained. "At Pewar, if we needed something all we had to do was ask the abbot Tenzeng Nyima. At Palpung, who do we ask? Poor old Shong-shong! And he doesn't even belong to this monastery! I've had lazy

Woodwork inside Palpung showing the effects of movement in the building.

workers at other places, but at least the people cared about conserving their building. Here, they don't."

But John wasn't a quitter. He called a meeting of all Palpung's monks. That afternoon, they assembled in the reception room, some seventeen maroon-robed lamas, most of them wrinkled old men. As they lowered themselves painfully onto cushions, I felt a jolt of embarrassment that we had the chutzpah to drag those sagacious ancients out of their nice warm quarters. But those guys needed waking up, and John was going to give it to them.

After some decorous preliminaries, John let them have it. Harry translated into Chinese; then Malu, who was proving an able and intelligent interpreter, translated into Tibetan. John berated the monks for Palpung's lack of cleanliness and for the lack of spirit. He told them what he was trying to do, what a great treasure they had in this spectacular building, how unique it was, and how proper conservation would bring Palpung to world prominence again. He said, "We can't repair and conserve Palpung alone; you can't do it alone; Shongshong can't do it alone; Situ Rinpoche can't do it alone. We all must work together."

"Any questions?"

Silence.

Then a voice. Shongshong's voice.

I don't know exactly what he said, because Malu and Harry declined to translate; and anyway the speech took long enough as it was. Shongshong went on and on in a low, sincere voice—reverently, humbly, unstoppably. With my smattering of Tibetan, I knew that he was relating the whole history of the monastery, who had built it, why and when, who had repaired, why and when and for how much money, what had happened during the Cultural Revolution, what had happened since, and how he, Shongshong, was ready to do his utmost in making it right again, making it a fit place for Situ Rinpoche to return to.

I was beginning to wonder how many more hours we might be trapped here when Shongshong reached a punctuation mark of some kind, and so we five started struggling to our feet, awkwardly, as our legs had gone to sleep from sitting for so long. The monks stared at us with grave attention as we staggered toward the door. How to get them to realize the meeting was over? At last I looked at them and said, "Ndro!" (Let's go!) Suddenly, the ice melted and they began moving and talking and getting to their feet also. Meeting adjourned.

Later, after dinner, John explained to me his plan of attack: "The first step is to set up a major survey, do a month of analysis, work out what the building's future use will be," he said. "We'll chop the whole thing up into a series of manageable annual projects. For each section, we'll strip out the earth to see the structure, then we'll undertake consolidation, replacement, and reconstruction. Probably five annual projects. It's daunting. But we can get it done."

Shongshong was way ahead of John on this score. Taking a piece of paper from John's notebook, he sketched a picture of how he felt the building should be divided up and attacked piece by piece, starting at the most dangerous area around the central courtyard. John looked over Shongshong's plan and pronounced it excellent.

However, before any actual work could begin, John and Razat would need to come again, this time for a longer stay, to draw up detailed plans. I sighed to think of how much money Wong How Man and I would have to raise.

It had now been eighteen days since we left Chengdu. Harry was laboring hard to carve a habitable niche out of Palpung's dust. ("I will teach these monks what is the meaning of *clean*!" he vowed). Assisted by the ever-helpful Malu, he created edible meals out of flour, butter, yak meat, and our dwindling store of imported comestibles. Nevertheless, John and especially Razat were feeling the homeward call.

There was, however, a problem about leaving. The telephone at the township headquarters was out of order, so if we rode out to the usual trailhead at Göncheshi, we'd have an uncertain hitchhike to town. But there was another way, a direct trail back, circumventing the highway. According to Shongshong, it was a seven-hour trip—just two hours longer than the usual route. It did, he cautioned, involve several passes.

My executive decision: Okay. Let's give a try.

By now it was November and frosty as our caravan climbed away from Palpung. Our guides, half a dozen local men and women, walked beside the horses, which carried team members and belongings. As we crested the first pass, the sun left us and snow began drifting down. Half an hour later we were walking in a blizzard. Stupidly, I had left my arctic outerwear packed inside my bag, now on another horse somewhere at the other end of the line. To ward off frostbite I dismounted and began to walk. But we were all still in high spirits, snapping photos of each other surrounded by swirling white. Harry was quite the horseman by now, twirling his rope and spurring his mount faster.

An hour or so later, as we left a straightaway and turned to descend into a valley, the sun came out, and with it a wave of euphoria. *"Taiyang chu laile!"* (the sun is out!) shouted Shongshong in a burst of uncharacteristic exuberance as the mist parted and we saw a stockade of peaks encircling a valley of stunning white. I was still walking, and what with my picture taking, was falling behind. The guides urged me onto the back of my white mare. We went on, trotting briskly beside a burbling river that was already leading us upward, to another pass.

At around one in the afternoon, we reached a cluster of stone shepherds' huts, deserted at this season. This was the lunch stop. By this time I was so cold that food seemed entirely beside the point. No one wanted to sit down on the rocky, deep-frozen ground. Standing, we chewed on some meat and bread, and Malu passed around a jar of arak. The liquor shot into my veins, warming my feet a degree or two. Ten minutes later we were on the move again.

Three more passes lay ahead: two at 4750 meters (15,700 feet) and one at 4700 (15,500). In between, there were rocks, more rocks, still more rocks, broad barren valleys full of rocks, and a nearly invisible trail. The mist closed in again, parting occasionally to show us blockbuster vistas of snow-covered ranges. As we were coming down from the second pass, Harry asked, "How much farther?"

"Two hours," Shongshong replied. "From the other side of the next pass you can see Derge." These were heartwarming words, for it's always better if you can see your destination, even if it's a hundred miles away. The trip was supposed to last seven hours, but already we were going on eight.

We rode an hour more. Summitting the last pass brought us to a valley where the air seemed warmer—but bitter disappointment, for there was no sign of the town. I asked Shongshong, "How much farther?"

"Two hours" replied the stoic Tibetan.

It's customary in Tibet to dismount when going downhill, so we got off our horses and walked, propelled by the happiness of civilization nearly in our grasp. Down down down we went, until at last we came to a solitary house, where we stopped for tea and snacks. The guides, who had been on foot all day, ate their tsampa ravenously. John and Razat were so eager to get back that they started ahead while the rest of us were still resting. Harry trotted after them, but took a wrong turn; a little later Malu and I spotted him on a lookout looking baffled. "What are you doing up there?" shouted Malu, laughing.

Not much later, Harry was on the trail beside me, making good time with both feet and mouth. "It's just like the Long March!" he said.

Shongshong riding across snowy highlands.

After eleven hours on the trail, we reached the outskirts of town. "*Ga ah te*" said villagers to Malu, giving the customary Derge greeting. Hard journey?

"*Ga ma te*" he lied. No, not hard.

That expedition, my first, had not been totally without problems. But we got the job done, and already in my head I was plotting our next trip.

Third Mission: 1995

CHAPTER 8

IN PEWAR'S paintings, each deity rests upon a throne made from a lotus, a flower revered in Egypt, India, Persia, China, and Central Asia. In nature, the lotus emerges from the murk of a stagnant pond, blooming in exquisite beauty and immaculate symmetry upon the dark water's surface. In the dharma, then, it represents immaculate conception, divinity, and freedom from karmic fault. Resting upon a lotus flower means overcoming concern for worldly gain or loss, renouncing the pollution of attachment that imprisons the unenlightened. To envision the lotus is to seek inspiration for the bold decision to emerge from the mire of worldly existence.

May 14, Kangding

This was a mission that almost didn't happen at all. First, there was a cash crisis when several prayed-for grants didn't come through. I had to cut the team, and the person that I cut was John Sanday himself. My reasoning was as follows: not only is Pewar in more desperate condition, but its monks are also more cooperative than those at Palpung. So after consultation with Wong How Man, I decided Palpung would have to take a back seat. At Pewar, however, the temple could not be repaired until we could save the upper murals, perilously hanging on to crumbling clay walls.

Little did I realize that saving Pewar's murals would be a colossal job, and that because of them, the art component of our conservation program would ultimately eclipse our original goal of conserving buildings.

It was at this critical turning point that our art conservation program began.

Next, there was—again!—a problem with the permits. Despite the fact that our host, the Sichuan Nationalities Research Institute, was a government unit, they just couldn't cope with the bureaucracy. I heard later that they had a bad reputation with other agencies, which would explain why their applications moldered at the bottom of the pile. Worse yet, they just didn't care. It was baffling, because most of their staff were ethnic minorities and many were Tibetan. But every time I went to see them, or tried to contact them from California, I got either a time-wasting runaround or no answer at all. Yet where else could I turn for help?

In Chengdu at the eleventh hour, with other team members about to arrive, I was on the verge of despair. Then a sympathetic member of the Institute took me to meet a fellow named Zhong Yang, who worked for an outfit called the Sichuan International Cultural Exchange Center. They are a quasi-government, quasi-private, for-profit company whose work is assisting international contact for Sichuan businesses and cultural groups—while at the same time monitoring that contact and reporting on it to government authorities. Perhaps because of their close relationship with law-enforcement groups, they had the connections to cut through the red tape. Incredibly, Zhong Yang promised that we'd have our permit in one week's time.

Based on Zhong Yang's pledge, I formulated the following plan: I'd bring the mural conservators to Kangding where they would give lectures on the principles of conservation, and we would look for apprentices to go with us to Pewar. Meanwhile, Zhong Yang would be pushing our paperwork through the mill in Chengdu. Somehow, our stamped papers would be brought to us in Kangding. Then we would proceed to Derge.

So there I was in Kangding with two very expensive Italian conservators (who had been recommended by John Sanday) taking a big gamble that things would somehow come together and we could go to Pewar. So far, the signs were good. We were setting Kangding afire, meeting all the notables in town who had anything to do with art.

People told us that western Sichuan had only a handful of ancient

murals left, all the others having been destroyed by weather, political turmoil, or ill-conceived attempts at repair. The Derge Printing House, for
example, lost paintings during the Cultural Revolution because the building was poorly maintained; moreover, fertilizers stored inside it caused
chemical damage to the murals.

It could have been much worse: according to some Derge friends, during the Cultural Revolution, local authorities were planning to plaster
over the Printing House murals, to secularize the building. For the short
term, the plaster would not have been catastrophic; but over the years,
alkaline components in it would have utterly destroyed the pigments.
Pewar Rinpoche, then under house arrest, heard of this plan, and luckily his influence was great enough that he was able to forestall it.

Later on, during repairs masterminded by Shongshong, paintings in
the Printing House's original lantern were lost because the walls underneath them had to be torn down. No one considered the possibility of
detaching the murals prior to demolition. Such technology had never
been seen on the Tibetan plateau.

As in Ganzi, the monasteries of Tibet Autonomous Region suffered
enormous losses, although a number of sites (such as the Potala Palace
and the Jokhang Temple) were largely spared. Through very unscientific
sampling of places visited on my random travels, I have seen what appear
to be ancient murals at a number of other locations in central Tibet—
more, certainly, than I have seen in Kham. Yet even in recent times, losses
continue. One acquaintance told of mural fragments observed in the rub-
ble generated by renovation of the Jokhang, Tibet's most sacred temple.
Since 1980, ill-advised repairs—not antireligious government policy—
have been the greatest enemy of Tibetan art.

In Kangding I met painter Nyima Tsering, who would become a sort
of godfather to the art conservation program. A Khampa born in Bathang
and raised in Derge, he is among the most successful Tibetan artists in the
world today. At 52 years old, he was handsome and compelling and
spoke eloquently in gorgeous Mandarin. He was working in a small studio on the fourth floor of a run-down building near the Kangding city
center.

"I have traveled all over the Tibetan plateau," he told us from behind a massive wooden desk. "I've looked at the way my people live, and I've looked at all kinds of Tibetan art. Monastery managers don't have a lot of education, so they don't understand the value of the old murals. They regard the paintings as an offering. The merit is in the making of them, not in their preservation."

His words brought to mind a nagging uncertainty about the whole basis for our conservation work. Tibetans believe in reincarnation: that all sentient beings—except for those lucky enough to achieve liberation—are caught up in an endless cycle of life, death, and rebirth. In an exercise that forcefully demonstrates the principal of impermanence, monks will spend weeks making an intricate sand mandala; then, in a climactic ceremony, they destroy their creation. It's a way of thinking that's alien to our materially oriented Western culture. So I had to consider: is it right to force our values on Tibetans by insisting that they preserve old buildings and murals? In the Tibetan context, wouldn't it be better to let the things die and be reborn again?

Nyima Tsering didn't think so. He said, "This is very important work you're doing. Ten years ago, I traveled around Tibet and saw many destroyed paintings. I reported this to the Panchen Lama[55] and he was very angry. He ordered all the monks to preserve the paintings. But it was too late. They just didn't know how. The government has hired experts from Beijing to protect the murals at the Potala Palace and Jokhang Temple, but unfortunately there are no Tibetans with this kind of skill."

My painter friend had been the lucky recipient of a broad education that included Western art through the Renaissance to modern times. In the Western sense, he was a highly enlightened and sophisticated Tibetan. He viewed Tibetan painting as an evolving art, not as a set of static traditions to be maintained without alteration. "In the West, five hundred years ago there was a transition: from entirely religious painting to art that included all kinds of subjects," he told me. "In Tibet, we are just now starting to walk that road."

---

55 The Panchen Lama is an incarnate teacher, traditionally equal to the Dalai Lama in religious authority but second in secular power. Nyima Tsering was referring to the previous incarnation, not the current, who is still a boy.

Nyima Tsering was a pioneer, taking Tibetan art in new directions. In his office I saw an easel carrying a large canvas. It was not at all like a Tibetan thanka with its rigidly prescribed traditional composition—instead it was an airbrushed watercolor in a style of fantastic realism. It

Nyima Tsering with painting of Tibetan envoys galloping across loess hills on their way to Mongolia.

showed a group of tiny horsemen galloping pell-mell through mountains of vast, barren loess. "This is Sakya Pandita and a party of Tibetans passing through Gansu on their way to Mongolia in the thirteenth century," he explained.[56] "I got the idea from a Ming Dynasty thanka. Their journey lasted three years. The original thanka didn't give any impression about the kind of terrain they passed through, the hardship they experienced. That's what I tried to express here."

56 His mission was to cement friendship between Mongolians and Tibetans. It was because of this friendship that the Mongols did not overrun Tibet, but instead became patrons of Tibet's Buddhist faith.

Nyima Tsering's dreams went far beyond his paintings. With several other prominent Tibetan intellectuals in Sichuan, he wanted to create a Tibetan Cultural Development Center, a think tank that would encourage advancement of medicine, philosophy, and art. But the government was uninterested in funding such a project, and so far it remained an illusive goal.

As we were getting ready to leave, Nyima Tsering told us he had a daughter, Deshi Yangjin, who was also a painter. He promised to send her to join our team as a conservation apprentice. He also promised to contact other people around town who would be interested in hearing my experts lecture about their work.

I later learned that Nyima Tsering had a mixed reputation among his fellow Tibetans. After he had labored for years as an obscure artist in a walled-off China, word of his talent began to leak outside in the late 1980s. In 1993, he was listed by the American Biographical Institute as a notable artist and invited to present his paintings at their annual meeting in Cambridge, Massachusetts. Foreign travel for Tibetans was extremely difficult, and Nyima Tsering's application was surely lubricated by his visibly pro-Beijing stance. He procured the treasured passport and an American visa, and he traveled to Boston for his first trip abroad.

During the small Cambridge exhibition, he received a phone call from the Chinese consulate in New York inviting him to show his paintings there to a larger, more prestigious audience. That event, which was attended by diplomats as well as the American press, was a big success. During one question-and-answer session, he was asked, "We've heard that Tibetan culture is in danger of destruction. What do you have to say about this?"

"Look at my paintings," Nyima Tsering replied smoothly, gesturing at the canvasses voluptuously decorated with mountain scenery, images from Tibetan folklore, Buddhist tales, village and monastic life, "and decide for yourself if Tibetan culture is in such danger."

This moment, recalled a friend, marked the beginning of the artist's upward climb.

Our lectures were given at Kangding's Tibetan School, a sort of junior college that offered three-year programs in Tibetan language, medicine, and painting. The headmaster was happy to provide facilities and the art students happy to attend. A couple of professors came from the nearby Kangding Guza Normal School, as well as Nyima Tsering and his daughter, Yangjin.

Not only that, but my telegram to Derge had resulted in Shongshong riding two days on the bus to Kangding to meet us. He brought with him another conservation apprentice, a pleasant, curly-haired young man called Aga. With rapidity that was astonishing for China, the stage for our lectures was set.

My experts were a husband-and-wife team, Carlo Giantomassi and Donatella Zari. They were the genuine article. They had trained at the elite Instituto Restauro Centrale in Rome and between them had 54 years of on-the-job experience. The first two pages of their resume gave an impressive list of Italian artworks they had restored, including paintings in the Vatican. The last two pages listed international credits: Ethiopia, Malta, Turkey, and ten other countries including, on one previous occasion, China. They were manifestly and abundantly qualified. Just as important: according to Sanday, they were good travelers.

On the morning of the fourth day, Donatella, Carlo, Harry, and I got into a taxi for the ride up to the Tibetan School, which overlooks the Dar River at the extreme northwest end of town. It was May, clear and bright as only the mountains can be, with the scent of spring flowers on the breeze. At the school, workmen were putting up a four-story "nouveau-Tibetan" building: concrete, with superficial Tibetan flourishes. We were ushered by the headmaster into its gray brick predecessor and upstairs to a classroom where our lectures would take place.

The students were ready for us. As soon as we entered, they all rose, chanted a greeting in unison, and bowed. I was completely charmed, but how to respond? Should I bow back? While I was standing there in befuddlement, Nyima Tsering sprang to my rescue, striding to the front and issuing a stream of Tibetan eloquence. When he came around to giving my Chinese name, Luo Bailian,[57] I broke in with an awkward sentence in

57 Luo is a common Chinese surname, derived from my surname Logan. Lian means "lotus" and comes from the Tibetan name "Pema," also meaning "lotus," bestowed by a Tibetan tutor long ago. Bai means "white."

Lhasa dialect, "My Tibetan name is Pema," and they all applauded. In a few more lines of only slightly more fluent Chinese, I explained the origins of our project. Then I turned the floor over to Donatella.

On came the slide projector, which, against all odds, had neither a burned out bulb nor a jammed mechanism; and the school had its own generator, so the electricity worked. Donatella began to show pictures of Italian paintings, mosaics, and statues. Harry translated her words into Chinese, in which the students were all fluent. Donatella soon lost everyone in the details of fresco, stacco, and lacunae. After half an hour, the students were glancing around and fidgeting. I wondered what, if anything, Tibetan kids could make of ten different renditions of the Madonna and Son? Could they see Tara, the female manifestation of compassion, in the Virgin's glowing face?

I feared we were losing our audience and brainstormed during lunch how to capture their interest. It occurred to me that what was missing was the *reason* for conservation. In the West, no one asks the question: why conserve? In Italy, for example, conservation is a glamour profession and aspiring conservators compete fiercely for places in the best schools. The urge to preserve our past is a deep-seated cultural value. I didn't know if Tibetans would instinctively feel the same way.

I scratched my head, jotted down ideas, and spent an hour looking up the Chinese words I would need. By the time we reconvened, I was ready with five reasons. One, for religion itself, because preservation of old art is a labor of great merit. Two, to show respect for ancient painters. Three, to learn their techniques. Four, to preserve a culture that is valued by the whole world. Five, because once the paintings are lost, they can never come back. Perhaps it was just the novelty of hearing Chinese come out of a foreigner's face, but at least I got their attention.

Then Carlo Giantomassi came on stage, and enraptured everyone with his amazing before-and-after photos. Dim, stained, soot-clad figures gave way to clean, bright ones. Centuries fell away like magic. I looked out into the crowd of faces and saw Shongshong. The old builder looked sorely out of place in the classroom full of young people. His face was blank, his eyes glazed, like those of an outsider having trouble making sense of things. He had been to Kangding only a few times before, and

Chengdu only once, I recalled. In cosmopolitan Kangding he was just another country bumpkin in a well-worn Tibetan coat redolent with yak butter. On the other hand, his friend Aga, 27 years old, was sitting straight up in his chair, eyes bright, eagerly taking it all in.

On the last day, Donatella and Carlo made a live demonstration. From the conservation supplies they had brought from Italy and Chengdu, they collected some solvents and cotton swabs and carried them to the school.

Carlo Giantomassi demonstrates cleaning technique on a thanka, while Yangjin films.

The teachers produced some ancient thankas: blackened, threadbare, and barely hanging together. The students, to my joy, crowded around eagerly to watch. The conservators did not have all the materials they would need to clean and reline a thanka, nor was there enough time for such an involved procedure. But they were able to mix up some solvents and apply them—ever so carefully to the thankas—rolling, not wiping, cotton swabs with excruciating care across the painted surface. The students jostled each other, angling for the best view.

After that smashing climax to our lectures, our spirits were high—everyone's, that is, except Harry's. I was planning to trade Harry for a Tibetan interpreter. His usefulness, I knew, declined the further we got from Chengdu, because he didn't really understand or respect Tibetans. He had been exposed to too much propaganda and said things like, "The reason Tibet is so backward is because of its religion." He wasn't getting on with Shongshong at all, and his Cantonese-accented Mandarin was hard for Sichuan people to understand.

I called Zhong Yang in Chengdu and learned that he had gotten our permits approved in record time. An emissary, Mr. Yuan,[58] arrived bearing our papers; he would accompany us throughout the trip. Besides Yangjin and Aga, we had acquired Fang, another apprentice.[59] There was just one more crucial addition to the team, a woman named Lhazom Dolma, who Malu had recommended and who would replace Harry as interpreter. She had been out of town when we arrived, working as a guide for a group of New Zealanders on a one-month trek of the Gongga Shan region.

One afternoon there was a knock on my hotel room door, and when I opened it I found Lhazom Dolma. She was thin and badly sunburned from her weeks in the mountains. She looked exhausted. "It was a difficult trip," she told me. "There was much snow, and the horses were not enough. The people all wanted to ride, but the leader, Margaret, would

58 Yuan was Tibetan, and bore the Tibetan name Yeshe Wangchuk although he rarely used it. A specialist in Tibetan history, Yuan was born in Liangshan Yi Autonomous Prefecture, southeast of Ganzi. This huge Yi enclave is home to some 50,000 Tibetans—a minority within a minority. Despite the large land area in Sichuan historically occupied by Tibetans, the Yi have a larger population in the province.

59 Fang was eager and available, but he was Chinese—not Tibetan—and for this reason I had doubts about accepting him. Unfortunately, however enthusiastic the Tibetan School students were, they could not leave Kangding in the middle of their semester. We needed helpers, and I had to take whomever I could get.

not let us hire any more horses. Of course I was only the interpreter, so I had to walk. I don't like trekking."

I assured her that when we went to Pewar she would have her own horse to ride. We were going there to do a job, not to push our personal envelopes.

"I must tell you something. Of course I want to go with you to Derge," Lhazom said. "But my contract with Margaret is not yet finished. I have to go with the New Zealand people back to Chengdu first. After that I will be free."

"But there's no time for that!" I exclaimed, dismayed. The trip to Chengdu and back would take at least three days. I couldn't keep my experts hanging around Kangding for that long, and public buses to Derge were so infrequent that if Lhazom didn't go with us, she would miss half the mission. Around here, English-speaking Tibetans are rare indeed—there was no way I could find another one in the few days that remained. I said, "Where is this Margaret? If I talk to her, and explain what we're doing, maybe she'll let you go early."

Lhazom was not optimistic, but she led me to the room where Margaret was staying. Margaret turned out to be a short, joyless woman of about 60, all gristle and business. "How do you do," she said, compressing my hand. "I'm Margaret, and I climb mountains."

I gritted my teeth and tried to smile as I introduced myself, explained my background, told her about the conservation program, and our plans for saving Pewar's murals. "That's all very nice," Margaret said curtly, "but what does it have to do with me?"

There was nothing to do but lay my cards on the table. I explained what I needed and offered her Harry in exchange for Lhazom. But Margaret wasn't having any of it. "No, no, no," she replied. "I've got a contract for one month and I don't want to change now."

I worked on her some more, appealing to her love of Tibetan culture, impressing her with my insider status, bribing her with names and phone numbers of my contacts in Derge so she could organize her own tours there—

"I run *treks*, not tours!" she interrupted crossly.

I corrected myself and continued, laying it on thick, fast, and heavy.

Harry stood by uneasily, watching himself being bargained over like a prize steer. In the end I got my way: Lhazom would go with us.

Lhazom Dolma had been born in India of exile parents. When her father grew old and fell ill, he decided that he would like to die in his homeland. Accordingly, he brought Lhazom, her sister, and her mother, back to Raga, their grassland home in the north of Derge. She was a teenager at the time. The Chinese government sent her to school for two years to learn Chinese, which she did brilliantly, mastering both standard Mandarin and the Sichuan dialect. But she was not assigned a job commensurate with her skills, because the government does not trust returned exiles in positions of responsibility. Now she was 25 years old, married to a local and living in Kangding but still feeling like an outsider.

I thought it would be smooth sailing now, but one more crisis was yet to emerge. The bus I had booked was broken down and nobody at the office where I hired it was interested in helping me find another, even at the grossly inflated rate I was ready to pay. Lhazom to the rescue. "I have a cousin-brother at the number one branch of the Kangding Transportation Company," she said. In a flash she was on the phone calling him. A car came out to fetch us to their office. Two hours later I was handing over the cash for a thirty-four-seat bus, which turned out to be half the price of the thirteen-seater we had before. "What kind of bus is this?" I asked.

"Don't worry," she replied. "It's new."

CHAPTER 9

ON PEWAR'S west wall, near the center, the following classic Jataka story
is told:

Once, in a kingdom lying in the foothills of the Himalayas, the Buddha was
born as a kind-hearted prince called Mahasattva. One year, a terrible drought
visited itself upon the kingdom, the people suffered greatly and many wild
animals died. Prince Mahasattva was walking in the woods with his two
brothers when they came upon a starving tigress and her seven cubs. The
cubs were barely alive, and the tigress was so feeble with hunger that she
could not even rise to give chase. Mahasattva's brothers quickly ran away,
but Mahasattva did not flee.

"I see from the suffering in your eyes and the frailness of your body that you
have been many days without food." he said to the sad, emaciated creature.
"What will you do?"

The tigress replied: "It is a terrible thing. My children are half dead. If I cannot find food soon, I must devour them so that at least one of us may live."

Remembering Buddha's teachings on selflessness, Prince Mahasattva replied:
"Take my body instead, for it is of little use to me." With that he laid down
before her. The tigress and her cubs devoured him, skin, bones, and all.
Thereafter they vowed to honor the prince's sacrifice by living virtuous lives.
Thus the forest was harmonious. The spot where the prince sacrificed himself is now marked with a stupa at Namobouddha in Nepal and is a site of
holy pilgrimage.

May 20

The next morning found my whole team riding in an oversized, not-completely-new-but-only-slightly-beat-up groaning, Leshan-brand lurcher, the kind that carries public transit passengers slowly but surely all over Tibet. The windows did close, and there were no springs poking out of the upholstery. I assuaged my conscience over the wasted space by picking up a few Tibetan hitchhikers as we went along. Lord knows in my backpacking days I had been given a ride or two.

After two days on the road, we reached Derge and moved on to Pewar by horseback in full daylight without incident.

Now, at last, I could sit back. It was time for somebody else to do the worrying. Donatella and Carlo unpacked their equipment and got down to work.

Originally, I had wanted them to do the whole job during this first trip. That job would include cleaning the lower murals and detaching the upper murals in preparation for demolition of the buckling upper walls. But long before they even got to China, the experts told me that I was dreaming. There was no way they could guess what equipment and materials they would need to detach murals they had not yet seen. Donatella, in her no-nonsense Italian accents, enunciated a cardinal principal of conservation: "It is impossible to say before. It depends on the color, the glue, the kind of wall material, and the dirt. So each time, we must test."

And test they did. The first task was to figure out how to clean the murals. Cleaning antique paintings, I learned, is like treating a sick old man: one must proceed cautiously, inspecting the results of every step. They spread a combination doctor's office and chem lab over the temple floor. We had bottles of solvent, tissue paper, gauze, cotton swabs, paint brushes, syringes, scalpels, and half a dozen different kinds of glue. Patiently, Carlo and Donatella tested various cleaning techniques, starting with plain water and then adding various solvents, drop by drop, to find the optimum elixir to separate color from dirt. The students—four of them now, for we had added one of Pewar's monks—asked lots of questions and made careful notes.

It soon emerged that our star pupil was Yangjin, Nyima Tsering's daughter.[60] She would become our top apprentice. At first blush, she seemed a cheerful and lucky girl who had every advantage. Her artist father had trained her as a painter; because of this, her own talent, and hard work, she had won a paying job in a unit of painters. Not only that, her work was attracting some notice.

But underneath, it seemed to me that Yangjin was having a hard time figuring out her place in the world. Her father, who doted on her, had grown up among Tibetans. He could mingle among them and speak the language fluently. But Yangjin had grown up in Kangding, where Chinese is the lingua franca of everyday life. Thus, she could understand Tibetan but could speak it only with great effort. Nevertheless, she enrolled in the Tibetan School of Sichuan, a bastion of ethnic pride where all classes are taught in Tibetan. There she was despised by many students, who felt that she had not earned her place but had won it only through her famous father. Whether her tenure at the school brought her closer to Tibetan society or pushed her further away is hard to judge.

Yangjin's trips with me to Derge proved to be an artistic watershed for her. Before, she had done little traveling on the Tibetan plateau, yet she had been struggling to produce canvases like her father's that expressed the heart and soul of her people, people whom she really did not know. After this first mission, however, Yangjin's muse would wake up. She would paint a series of new, vibrant works based on her experiences in Derge. She later told me, "I want to travel more, all over Tibetan areas, so I can understand people's lives and develop my painting." The tragedy was, even as she was trying to understand her people, they would not accept her. She was smart and talented, but perhaps would have been luckier to have had different parents.

Yangjin and Fang were great apprentices, but the monk provided to us by Pewar was hopeless. His eyes would wander all around the room even while he was daubing solvent on a mural.

We did have one more promising student: Aga. I learned that Aga was both a painter and a doctor of Tibetan medicine, which explained his

60 Fang was also very good, but did not work with us again after this mission.

patience and sensitivity. He quickly became everyone's favorite, what with his aptitude for foreign languages and his quixotic personality combination of bashful boy/wise doctor.[61] The two young women, Lhazom Dolma and Yangjin, teamed up to torment him with nonstop flirtation. "A supremely happy being," I wrote in my journal, "a pleasure to be around."

Aga performs pulse diagnosis on a patient in Pewar's courtyard.

Morale was fantastic. We had gelled beautifully as a team. Pewar's hospitality was boundless; the goofy old concierge monk Tsetra was seeing to our every need. Mr. Yuan, the government emissary, was resourceful, humorous, and completely at home in a Tibetan setting. We all learned some Italian. The late-May weather was brilliant. We had brought plenty of good food. Nobody got sick. And best of all, the work was going well.

The lantern of Pewar held three walls covered in murals. The fourth wall—on the south—held a large window admitting sunlight to the temple below, a typical arrangement for a Tibetan temple. The west wall, although painted, had already succumbed some years ago; it bore new,

61 Aga had always lived in Derge, and was so thoroughly Tibetan in character and habit that I was quite astonished to learn, some years later, that his father is Han Chinese.

90

poorly done murals, not worth saving. Each of the remaining two "good" walls held murals 2.6 meters high by 8.2 meters long. There was also a strip of painted surface 30 centimeters wide on the south wall, between the window and the corner. Carlo and Donatella selected this place, which was decorated with a column of Sakyamunis, for their first test.

Standing on scaffolding eight meters above the temple floor, the two conservators cleaned a poster-sized section of wall. This itself was an involved procedure. They tried various weak solvents, working with painstaking care. The blue-green pigments, blackened and fragile, were most difficult to clean.[62] The reds, oranges, and whites were stronger and glowed brightly after just a few treatments. The conservators rarely applied their tools directly to the paintings; rather, they held a sheet of Japanese tissue paper over the mural and used a paintbrush to apply liquid over it so the paper would stick. After a few minutes, they peeled the tissue paper from the wall, removing a thin layer of dirt. Then they repeated the procedure. I soon realized that if you were fussy and careful enough, cleaning even one mural could take a lifetime.

After cleaning the test section, they prepared it for detachment by painting it with clear fixative to protect the color. Then they applied two layers of gauze and glue. In between steps they had to wait for the section to dry completely, and even in good weather this took a full day. But the time was not wasted; for the conservators had four students to teach, and we had a lot of murals to work on.

Downstairs, by the temple entrance, were two alcoves that normally would be decorated with painted images of the four Guardian Kings, a motif found in Buddhist temples all over Asia. However, at Pewar, the alcoves walls were covered with mud, leaving not a clue as to their contents. It was just the sort of project to challenge conservation students and keep them busy. Carlo and Donatella set the apprentices to work lifting layer after layer of dirt. "*Women gei pusa xizao*" remarked Yangjin cheerfully as she used a brush to tease up a bit of mud: We're bathing the gods!

From Shongshong's mental archives we managed to extract some important facts about the old paintings—that the white layer beneath

62 See Appendix II for a list of pigments and the materials used to make them.

the paint is kaolin (the same clay used to make porcelain), and that the gloss on the images comes from stone polishing—that is, burnishing the finished painting with agate, coral, horn, or some other smooth, hard stone. These facts ought to have been simple to uncover; but with Shongshong, direct questions rarely worked. Carlo asked about the material under the paint, and suddenly Shongshong wanted to talk about the ceiling. Our first five inquiries about the murals' shiny surface brought the answer, "because there is gold and silver in there."

Conservators and apprentices clean the Guardian King murals at the entrance to Pewar Monastery's main temple.

While the art conservation was going on, I held meetings with Pewar's abbot, Tenzeng Nyima, to discuss repairs to the building. The word "abbot" conveys a picture of surpassing wisdom and stern authority. But Pewar was a small, poor, underpopulated monastery, and Tenzeng Nyima was more reluctant administrator than charismatic sage. For a Tibetan, he was a really big guy, tall with broad shoulders, beefy hands, and colossal feet. Although strong as a bear, he was a gentle chap—even for a monk. Like Shongshong, he always spoke quietly. "I was born in Ebi township of Jomda county," he told me once, when I asked him about his life. The area he named is farm country, across the Dri Chu in Tibet Autonomous Region. Customarily, Pewar draws most of its manpower from this district.

When Tenzeng Nyima was a boy of about 10, his leg was crippled by an accident, the right foot twisted sideways. Of course there was no doctor to set the bone; nevertheless after many months he was able to rise from his bed and walk again, albeit with a pronounced limp. Unable to do heavy farm work, he took up the study of Buddhism. "I first studied with my uncle, Lore Simei, who was also Pewar Rinpoche's teacher," he told me. "I studied at home until I was fifteen; then I came to Pewar."

In normal times, young men with physical defects are not admitted to monasteries; but Tenzeng Nyima's application came when Pewar was newly reopened and in desperate need of manpower. That, his high aptitude, and his personal connection to Pewar Rinpoche through their shared teacher assured his entry.

I first met Tenzeng Nyima in 1991, when he was a bright-eyed 26-year-old. Then, he had been abbot for only three years. Since then I had watched him age: his stomach pressing outward, his face going jowly. Tibet's poor diet, harsh conditions, and the pressures of leadership had aged him twice the number of years that had passed. Tenzeng Nyima was tired of the endless problems of running a monastery; he just wanted to pass on the baton and go back to a life of contemplation. But that wasn't going to happen anytime soon.

Now I was meeting Tenzeng Nyima to obtain something crucially important: the accounting records for Pewar's repairs. This I had to see, and it had to make sense, and I had to be able to report it to project sponsors; otherwise we would not get funds to continue. So here I was having a meeting with Tenzeng Nyima as chief accountant, Lhazom as translator, and Shongshong as, well, Shongshong, for the old Tibetan builder had his hands in everything we did.

Our meeting was not really a meeting, it was an audit, and I was the evil auditor. Tenzeng Nyima and Shongshong wore the same nervous smiles worn by auditees the world over. The concierge monk Tsetra stood by to ensure that no mishap would befall his friends owing to tea short-age. Lhazom the translator sat with us. And so we were ready to start.

Tenzeng Nyima untied a bundle of yellow silk, and out spilled a pile of cigarette-rolled papers and odd bits of origami onto the table. These were the monastery's financial records. One by one, we opened each lit-tle paper unit, which was a folded stack of tissue-thin receipts in various sizes.

Some were the forms mandated by the Chinese government, neatly filled out and smudged with carbon on the back. These are the most solid receipts you can get, but merchants don't like to use them because they prefer to keep profits off their official books. On the next level down from real receipts were informal notes scrawled on ordinary paper but authenticated with a real chop. This is what shops like to give, and we had quite a lot of them. Most dodgy of all were bits of notepaper hand-written in Tibetan script and certified by a scrawl or a red thumbprint. That's what we got from laborers, for you can hardly ask for a carbon copy invoice from an illiterate carpenter.

What the Internal Revenue Service would make of such documents was beyond imagining. Nevertheless, I would take these papers home with me and file them in our official records.

Here's what they were buying. According to last year's plan, Tenzeng Nyima and Shongshong were to acquire a tractor, build a road from Pewar to the forest, get permits for tree cutting, fell the trees, and mill the timber in preparation for construction. Shongshong had a notebook in which he had recorded these expenses, grouped according to no dis-cernible system. Tenzeng Nyima had a notebook of his own whose pages had been preprinted with the English "NAME," "ADDRESS," and "TEL." These he found it to convenient to ignore, covering the paper with great flourishing curls of *U-mei* script.

I got out my calculator and started checking their sums. They were, I discovered, mostly wrong. It would all have to be done over. We went through every piece of paper and every figure. Lhazom translated while Tenzeng Nyima and I simultaneously punched individual calculators. In the end I recorded the total in my notebook, and Tenzeng Nyima signed it, verifying it as accurate.

Tenzeng Nyima's accounts became, for me, a window into the life of his monastery and village. For instance, unskilled laborers—the folks who toted clay and water, and hefted timbers—got 15 to 20 yuan per day, that is, around U.S.$2. By contrast, a carpenter's daily wage was 35 yuan, plus the employer was expected to supply meals (potatoes, noodles, pork, cooking oil). I learned not to blink at line items for beer, which is routinely awarded for overtime, and cigarettes, a vital social lubricant. Our long-suffering tractor accounted for 1,483.54 yuan worth of parts and repairs, not counting the replacement engine (2,980 yuan). Our tractor driver, who was also our tractor mechanic, had the most regular employment (16 yuan/day), and got food in addition. In 1997, we would have to replace him after he got into a fistfight (123 yuan, medical expense).

When we were done with the books, we moved on to upcoming work. Really, I wanted to prevent Shongshong from going very far with the repairs on Pewar's temple, because when John Sanday came back he would surely have his own ideas how to go about it. Besides, we couldn't touch the lantern and roof until the upstairs paintings were detached, probably next year. Shongshong was impatient, but because I held the moneybags, he had to hold off. Anyway, there was plenty of other work to do.

Shongshong's plan was to shore up the temple's foundation by building a low wall of cemented stone blocks around the outside. I wasn't too happy about this, because it would alter the monastery's appearance; but without John Sanday there I couldn't think of any arguments against it, so I agreed. Shongshong also wanted to rebuild most of the U-shaped courtyard wing, which was in dire straits since the 1993 earthquake. Pewar Rinpoche had sent some money to construct living quarters, a toilet, kitchen, and—most incredibly—a shower; but Shongshong needed more from me to finish the job. He had devised a clever way to separate toilet drainage from the footpath that would serve circumambulating pilgrims. New ditches would prevent hill runoff from damaging the foundation. He took me around the outside of Pewar, outlining what he had in mind.

All in all, it was an ingenious plan. Shongshong even had prepared a cost estimate. Including materials, wages and various other expenses such as transportation, they would need U.S.$8,000 for the work. I sat down and totaled up my resources: money stashed in various accounts in Hong Kong, Chengdu, and Derge, leftover expedition funds, money that was expected from U.S. donors. It was just about enough. I told him to go ahead.

Workers constructing new living quarters attached to Pewar.

So much for paperwork. The fun part of my job was watching the experts and their helpers at work. After three days of applying cloth and glue to the test section, the moment of truth came. We all held our breath as they seized one corner of the section and carefully pulled on it until the whole thing came off like stiff wallpaper. When it was free we saw that the clay had separated cleanly, and no color was left behind. The test was a success!

CHAPTER 10

ON THE WALLS of Pewar's anteroom are the Four Great Kings, guardians of Buddhist temples across east Asia. To the right of Pewar's entrance, guardians of the East and North stand beside the heavy double doors; guardians of West and South face them. The style of painting is totally unlike Pewar's interior: the Great King's shapes are suggested not by outlines, but by blocks of vigorous red and white aloft on a black background.

These Maharajikadeva abide on Mount Meru where they protect the gates to Tushita Heaven; they also defend the dharma and its followers from marauding asuras.

The images are damaged and obscured by mud. The eastern guardian, Dhritarashtra, King of Celestial Musicians, is the most discernible, standing just to the right of Pewar's temple entrance. A stout, Bacchanalian figure, he wears white-soled boots, robes trimmed in gold, a headpiece of flames. His delicate fingers pick at a lute carried in his hands.

May 30

Our Pewar mission was finished, and I decided that the team would go to Palpung for a couple of days before heading back to Derge. In late spring sunshine, the horseback ride up the Bei Chu was ecstasy—we laughed all the way there. But the monastery's gloomy reception room hit us like a douse of cold water. We sat silently, munching the victuals the monks had laid out.

Palpung's abbot came to greet us. He was an august lama of about 65, a tall, handsome Khampa, and I imagined that hearts must have broken all over eastern Tibet when he first took vows as a monk. Khepa Tsering, as he was called, combined the mien of a learned master with a Tibetan's sly humor and a teacher's big heart. We traded speeches. The abbot wel-

Team traveling by horse caravan from Pewar to Palpung.

comed us, but he could not hide his frustration that so little had been done for his monastery. "Please, please get Palpung repaired soon," he begged, adding that Situ Rinpoche had forbidden him to retire before the repairs were done. More weight on my shoulders, I thought, sighing. I had explained about our decision to concentrate resources on Pewar, but this didn't relieve my guilt.

I learned from Shongshong that Akong Rinpoche had visited last winter, bringing a 10,000-yuan donation. Akong Rinpoche is an influential Kagyu incarnate lama who lives in Scotland and has a great many students there and around the world. Every year he comes to Tibet loaded with cash that he spreads around in a lot of small donations, mostly to schools. Akong Rinpoche's donation to Palpung amounted to less than U.S.$1200, but it would keep a little bit of work going.

In late afternoon, I decided to leave the building and go check the experimental crack repair that John Sanday had made in another building the previous year. I went alone, walking out of the east door and around the main temple in proper clockwise fashion, as I had done dozens of times before. As I rounded the toilet there was a dog crouching a few meters away, growling.

What's eating him? That was a good question, but I didn't consider it further. Although Palpung's dogs were filthy, vile critters, they had never molested me.

Alas: fatal mistake.

The moment I passed him and my back was turned, the thing sprang. I saw nothing, only heard a roar and felt something come at me. I spun around to face him: a raging whirlwind of teeth, jaws, and violent carnivorous movement. *This can't be happening!* I thought, but only for a moment, for it was happening fast and all too horribly real.

One thing about dogs: any show of weakness only makes them fiercer. Running away was out of the question. "Shitdamnyougetoutofhere!" I screamed but the mutt didn't back off. Instead, he lunged again.

"Shitohshitohshit!" I don't know what I was saying, but the thing was still snarling and snapping. I began to kick, but my heavy boots only seemed to egg him on.

"Shitohshitdamnhelphelp!" Now the rest of the pack was coming: mangy Tibetan mastiffs, lean, savage, and ugly as sin. They quickly closed in around me, snapping at my feet and baying like mad. I had no weapons, and there was no one else around. It was far too late to throw rocks, which is what I should have done in the first place.

Time passed: perhaps only seconds but it felt like eternity. I was still kicking hard, for if I stopped for even a moment, there would be a dozen fangs in my flesh. My kicking was enraging them, and in the pandemonium of half a dozen yowling, plunging animals, a few teeth sunk home. I was too terrified to notice.

Moving backwards, suddenly I tripped over a rock and went down. For some reason, the dogs didn't circle, they stayed at my feet, which were now bike-pedaling like mad.

"Aaaaaah!" I screamed, and kept my feet moving. But now I was getting tired. At 3950 meters (12,959 feet) above sea level, my wind couldn't last much longer.

Just then monks began streaming out of the monastery. They picked up rocks and hurled them at the dogs, who now retreated, howling. When the beasts had been driven off, I let my legs fall to the ground. I lay there exhausted and heaving, sucking thin air into my lungs.

The monks gathered around, tsk-tsking at my improvidence. I slowly got to my feet and pulled up trouser legs to reveal gashed calves and rivulets of blood. Some of the blood was coming from above the knee, but I wasn't about to take off my pants in front of a bunch of monks to identify the precise source. Still panting heavily, I retrieved my battered camera from the ground and hobbled oh so slowly inside.

Dusk had just fallen, and the monastery was dark. I limped through Palpung's labyrinth of stairwells and corridors feeling like the lonely hunchback keeper of a haunted mansion. Upstairs I went to where the team was awaiting dinner.

"I've been attacked by dogs," I announced in the doorway, flashed a bit of gory leg at them, then hobbled straight to the room that I shared with the three other women. They rose, shocked, then followed me inside. We slid the door closed.

Now I could take off my pants without offending Asian decorum. To my dismay I discovered high on my inner thigh a cavernous oozing hole.

There was one name on everyone's lips: Aga. With the medical training he had received from his father, he was, perforce, our expedition doctor.

The fellow was not around; he had stepped out to pay a call on one of his many girlfriends hereabouts, for he had grown up in a house below Palpung and was well known in the neighborhood. While we waited for him to be summoned, Yangjin and Lhazom went into a tizzy of preparation, bustling around, boiling water and fetching the expedition medical kit.

Aga appeared, and the room suddenly calmed. *The doctor is here, and he'll know what to do*, was the new theme. Aga was carrying a well-worn leather satchel marked with a red cross. He washed his hands and took a long look at my wounds—especially the one on my upper thigh.

Seeing his slyly exaggerated interest, Yangjin and Lhazom burst out laughing in spite of themselves.

Aga cracked a knowing smile. Then he went to work.

Let me be frank here: I'm a fan of Tibetan culture, but Tibetan medicine fills me with misgiving. To my mind, it's just around the corner from voodoo. But here I was bleeding, and there was Aga looking calm and professional. I decided that for such a classically Tibetan malady as dog-bite, I might as well be treated by Tibetan methods.

Recumbent and trouserless, I watched doubtfully as Aga unpacked his bag. On the one hand, he had reassuring white boxes in which forceps, syringes, and glass bulbs of penicillin were neatly packed; on the other—and more disturbing—hand, he had little drawstring leather bags full of (I imagined) elixirs and potions. Just what was he going to do?

Bypassing the mystical-looking leather bags, Aga took some disinfecting powder and mixed it with hot water in a tea bowl. Then he cleaned my wounds. I watched in morbid fascination as he used forceps to push cotton balls deep inside my leg, then withdraw them. Blood flowed, copiously. In the middle of it all, I remembered why the dogs guard the toilets so zealously: they eat human excrement.

Suddenly I began to feel queasy.

Aga finished by stuffing the wounds with antibacterial-soaked gauze. He injected me with painkiller and antibiotic, coated me with iodine, sprinkled me with powder, and wrapped me with gauze. I was awarded a bucket full of pills: amoxycillin, vitamin C, and something called lao-han that tasted like peppermint and was supposed to be beneficial to the blood. Then the doctor disappeared into the night.

Nighttime was not restful. I couldn't find a comfortable position. The dogs outside yowled. Hearing them, I relived the attack half a dozen times. I was deeply, primally unsettled, an alpha female suddenly cast down to the bottom of the food chain, transformed into naked prey. Rats scurried around the room, throwing Yangjin into a tizzy. I thought, how can she make such a fuss about a few rats when I've got dog poison in my veins?

Sunrise was a great relief. I ate my breakfast tsampa regally immobilized in bed. Lamas came to pay convalescent calls. Aga came to check up on me, holding my wrist for pulse diagnosis, while Yangjin and Lhazom looked on a little enviously.

The indomitable Shongshong arrived with a couple of monks to go over accounts, for I had given Palpung money for some minor work. Then I had to get up and meet some township officials. My wounds began to leak, and Aga was called in to clean and rebandage them. But after that was done, dinner was absolute silliness; I laughed so hard I thought my bandages would burst.

The next day we rode five hours over Nyingo La and nGosen La to the trailhead at Göncheshi, where a couple of cars picked us up. Upon reaching Derge, I was taken to the town medical clinic, a sad, dilapidated place. Here began what would be a month-long daily exercise, in whatever city I happened to be, of locating a doctor to change my bandages and clean my wounds. The Derge doctor, a smiling Tibetan in a felt hat, had a chipped enamel tray laid out with instruments and wretched-looking mug of iodine, but he got the job done. To top it off, he supplemented the arsenal of drugs Aga had prescribed with a few of his own favorites.

After Derge lay that familiar homeward road: over Tro La, through dusty Manigango and rambunctious Kandze, onward toward Kangding. In every town there was a clinic and often an adjustment in my prescriptions, for as we headed back to civilization the doctors grew progressively more knowledgeable—or at least that's what they said. In Kangding we dropped off everyone except the two conservators and Mr. Yuan. Only one day of driving remained to Chengdu.

At 6 A.M. we started out, swiftly plummeting to the Dadu River, then climbing again through spruce forest to the last summit, Two Wolf Pass, at 3000 meters (9843 feet). After Kangding, one sees nothing of Tibet, just roadside cafes, rustic truck stops, and Chinese peasants tilling vegetables. I had taken my pills, and now they were taking me; I couldn't stay awake. An hour or so after Two Wolf Pass, I noticed groggily that the car had stopped.

Ah, I thought: a delay. How nice—now I don't have to be slammed around while napping. Back to sleep.

Some time later I came to and noticed that we still weren't moving. What's the problem, anyway? *"Kuafang"* replied Mr. Yuan. Landslide.

Oh. Back to sleep.

Woke up again. Landslide? Hmmm. Could be bad. I eased myself out of the car and walked forward to the front of the stopped traffic. The highway was single-lane here, dynamited out of a vertical wall of jungle-covered mountain. Picturesque waterfalls poured down from on high. About 75 meters below the road was a burbling stream cutting between stone cliffs. We were only some twenty cars behind the front of the line.

Heaped on the tarmac was a pile of rocks. I couldn't see the other side because the road had a hairpin turn here; but the pile didn't seem very large to me. A cluster of people stood there staring helplessly at the disaster. Why weren't they picking up rocks? Stupid, fatalistic Chinese! I was just thinking of hefting a few stones over the precipice when I saw another load of debris tumble down and clatter to the base of the pile. The crowd jumped back, me with them. But a minute later they were edging closer again, daring each other, laughing nervously with the carefully measured bravado of people standing beside a murmuring volcano. So, there was a standoff.

The rest of the day passed in drug-induced haze. Time stopped. I took naps, rising occasionally to go and check the rock pile. As always, no change. Carlo, Donatella, Mr. Yuan, and the driver kept themselves occupied somehow. Once I hiked backward, uphill toward Two Wolf Pass, but the line of cars was endless. It was impossible for anyone to turn around. There must be a thousand cars and five thousand people trapped here by now.

Peasants materialized out of nowhere to sell biscuits, boiled eggs, and instant noodles at grossly inflated prices. Litter accumulated by the roadside. One truck driver pulled the canvas down from his load to make an awning. A group of men was squatting on the shoulder playing cards noisily. Those who had a fire and kettle shared their hot water with those who didn't. People visited back and forth. There was no sign of anyone official. In America, a disaster like this would have had the Red Cross out within hours bringing blankets and provisions. Here, there was nothing.

I found a gang of Khampas, truckers from Chamdo, sitting around a small fire and sucking tea from a dirty jar. Their Tibetan coats were stained and dusty. Some of them wore Khampa red tassels. Ah, home! I sat down with them. Suddenly I started to feel alive again. I had some of

The descent from Two Wolf Pass toward Chengdu
is often blocked by landslide.

their tea. An English tourist wandered by. He had just been to Kangding, but understood nothing. "Who are the guys with red stuff in their hair?" he asked. "Are they Tibetans?"

In late afternoon a couple of wiry Chinese in hardhats arrived to clamber up into the brush above the slide. The rumor came back that there was a huge boulder up there, ready to tumble, and this was why no bulldozer dared go near the pile. I took a look, and saw a boulder big enough to flatten any bulldozer like a Road Runner and Wile E. Coyote cartoon. Our rescuers, who were either brave or desperate or both to take this kind of work, were getting ready to set a charge that would blow the boulder loose. They ran a long wire to one side, and word was passed around the crowd to get back. We did. Then came an enormous POW! that crashed up and down the canyon. Carlo went out to see the result and came back to report that the rock pile was bigger, but the boulder hadn't moved.

The driver and Mr. Yuan went off to sleep in other vehicles, leaving the Land Cruiser in custody of the conservators and myself. At least we had sleeping bags. We folded down the rear seat. Carlo gallantly let us ladies stretch out in back, while he slept behind the wheel.

I slept soundly until 5 A.M., when the last of the drugs cleared my system and I knew what I had to do.

First step: find Mr. Yuan. I walked forward, peering into all the cars at their sleeping occupants. He was half a dozen vehicles forward. I told him what I had in mind. His reply was simply, "Let's go."

Second step: After briefing the others and collecting a few supplies, Mr. Yuan and I went to the rock pile. We gazed up at the cliff, which was still sending down occasional showers of debris. We took a deep breath, then ran, pell-mell, over the stones to the other side. When I got around the corner, I saw that the rock pile was much, much bigger than I had imagined. It was like a house full of stones had fallen on top of the road— a transit catastrophe of epic proportions. I knew then that I was doing the right thing.

Third step: This was unexpectedly easy. On the other side of the pile we found a waiting bus. It was full of peasants and their sacks, crates, and animals. Several windows were broken. Most of the seat covers showed carefully hand-sewn patches. It was beautiful. A few minutes after we boarded, it started moving.

Fourth step: After a couple of hours we reached Ya'an, a good-sized city. Unfortunately, it was Sunday, and offices were closed. The resourceful Mr. Yuan scouted around, however, until he found someone with a car who was willing to go back and pick up the conservators and our baggage. Peasants would be hired at whatever amount of money it took to carry the bags over the rock pile. As for the driver, there was little we could do except send back food for him and pray for his early release.

In the end, after a long, long day, we made it to Chengdu that night. Another mission done!

Fourth Mission: 1996

CHAPTER 11

BENEATH Pewar's paintings is a band of dark blue decorated with a simple repeating motif, a chain of *dorjes*, or thunderbolt scepters, painted in gold brushstrokes. The word *dorje* in Tibetan means "lord of stones," referring to the indestructibility and brilliance of diamond. The Sanskrit name, *vajra*, originally referred to lightning wielded by Indra.

When used in ritual, the dorje is held in the practitioner's right or masculine hand. The dorje is usually paired with a bell, which signifies wisdom and is held in the left or feminine hand. Together, they represent perfect joining of skillful means with discriminating awareness.

At the center of the dorje is a sphere sealed by the syllable HUM, whose three letters symbolize freedom from causation (*hetu*), freedom from conceptual thought (*uha*), and the groundlessness of all dharmas (*m*). The five double prongs represent the Ten Perfections: generosity, morality, renunciation, wisdom, energy, patience, truthfulness, determination, loving-kindness, and equanimity. Together the components are a weaponlike object manifesting eternal truth.

April 21, Chengdu

Three babes on a shopping spree! That's what we were: myself, my friend Lily Zhang, and our driver, the fashionable Ms. Lie. We shopped until we dropped, tooling around Chengdu in a whopping big Land Cruiser provided by a sponsor.[63] But what strange goods! Xylene and

63 The New China Hong Kong Group, Limited. It had been their car and driver, too, who was trapped with the team at Two Wolf Pass as described in the previous chapter.

silica gel, eyedroppers and aspirating bulbs, screwdrivers and trowels. We trekked the length of Red Star Boulevard, stopping in hardware stores, electric shops, and a chemical supply house. Lily, who was Harry's wife, smiled sweetly at the shopkeepers as she bargained in her native Chengdu dialect, while I pointed and stammered my bad Chinese at the merchandise.

This would be my biggest, longest, most difficult mission yet. I had a huge list of conservation tools and materials to buy for the conservators, more lists of food, medical supplies, household sundries, and packing materials. The number of people to feed and equip was somewhere between twelve and twenty—I didn't yet know for sure. We would need to keep ourselves and our work going in isolation at Pewar Monastery for nearly a month. I had five days to get everything ready. It was fast, frantic fun.

Chengdu was like an old home to me by now, for I had passed through here many times before. Sensations wrapped around me like a comfortable cloak: honking horns and tinkling bicycle bells; pots of chili-fired stew bubbling at restaurant doorways; pedicab drivers snoozing on the passenger seats; the rapid, voluble, argumentative strains of Sichuan-*hua*; haze hanging in the air like the city was suspended in a cloud. Yet much was changing, too. The words "development," "reform," and "opening" were on everyone's lips, in newspaper headlines, painted in huge block characters on the sides of walls and buildings. China was rocketing forward.

At 5:30 P.M. my two comrades wanted to go home to their children, so I bid them farewell and forged on alone. Thinking of team morale, I bought badminton rackets, a chess set, and a suction-cup throwing game. The next day, all day long, I was running my hands over screwdrivers, pulleys, paint thinner, chopsticks, hand drills, paper cups, dish soap, files, tweezers, and washbasins. I saw things we needed in almost every store. Money poured between my fingers.

We went to the discount food district, an alley lined with tiny, over-stuffed shops. We arrived just at closing time. Most shops had rolled down their doors, but we found one still open. The owners' eyes got wide and very bright as I filled up box after box with bright-colored, plastic-

packed, flavor-enhanced snacks. The neighbors decided to stay open a little longer, and sure enough, soon I was spending twice as much over
there. Then the doors of other shops started rolling back up, and I went
pawing through boxes of sausage rolls, M&Ms, and chewy fruit sticks,
all in crumbling, guaranteed-to-disintegrate-after-one-use cartons stacked
to the ceiling in one-room warehouses. I bought dozens of cans of meat
and fish. I bought biscuits by the stack. We were looking at Sichuan pick-
les when it began to close in on eight o'clock and we were starving, and
I had an appointment at nine, so we had better leave.

We went to a restaurant where Ms. Lie's husband worked and pigged
out. Then we drove all the boxes to the Sichuan International Cultural
Exchange Center. We banged on the door until Chao the groundskeeper
came and helped us carry all the stuff upstairs. There would be many,
many more loads to come.

The next day, we went to a hospital warehouse to get five kilos of
cotton and many hundred meters of gauze. With the help of a saleslady,
we scrutinized the medical kit shopping list, striking out items unavailable in Chengdu and adding some traditional Chinese medicines. Then
back to the chemical supply house for more toxics and flammables. And
so it went.

Lily did quite a bit of shopping on her own, coming back with sacks
of onions, garlic, ginger, chili, MSG, and the mouth-numbing, soap-tast-
ing pepper called *huajiao*—spices without which no Sichuan person could
possibly be content. I biked around town, meeting supporters and team
members definite and supposed, inspecting buses, and canvassing banks
for the best exchange rate. Receipts stacked up: tissue paper with carbon-
paper black characters dancing on narrow red lines, all of which would
have to be translated and listed and added before the end.

For the last round of shopping, Lily and I went to look at bulk rice,
beans, and flour in their multitude of types and grades. Our purchases
were calculated in tens of kilos. Salespeople adored us. Whipsaw Sichuan-
hua had my head spinning, and what would I have done without gentle-
voiced Lily to play my cards for me? In her miniskirt and heels, she was
the consummate bargainer. We grabbed some honey on the way back, but
decided to skip the sugar and buy it in Kangding.

The personnel list shifted daily. My new hosts provided an efficient, round-faced, city Tibetan named Denba Dargye to accompany us; he showed up to our first meeting in a dapper gray suit. After many calls to Kangding, I determined that last year's wonderful interpreter, Lhazom Dolma, had vanished. Harry was at university in England. I found an English-speaking Tibetan girl, but her boss refused to let her take the time off. I lined up a Chinese man, but at the last minute he backed out. What a roller coaster of a week it was!

Then it transpired that Two Wolf Pass, the place where Carlo, Donatella, and I had been trapped last year, had now been reorganized. It was still one way, but instead of shifting directions twice daily, now it was one way all day, every day, going up on odd days and down on even, so my planned departure date would have brought us smack into a road-block. I tried to hurry, but suddenly the conservators had some fiberglass that they desperately needed (why wasn't it on the list?) that wouldn't be ready to pick up for another day, so okay, we slip a whole two days. Call everyone. Rebook the bus. Pay the new hotel bill. Calculate the new schedule. Send telegrams to Kangding and Derge.

The day of departure was amazingly smooth. We were even ready early, as I allowed a generous four hours for packing the bus. And then we were buzzing down the road, me in the front, in my seat of honor next to the driver. I immediately fell asleep.

We arrived in Kangding a day and a half later, after a much-too-long surmounting of Two Wolf Pass, which exemplifies the principle that in China things always get much, much worse before they get even the slightest bit better. That road had been under repair—for what, three years?—and it was still *much* slower than it had been during the good old days when it was unrepaired.

Kangding itself was completely torn up due to ongoing repair of damage from the previous summer's flood. At least they had given up the notion of covering up the Tseto River and putting buildings on top of it— an ominous rumor I had heard on my last visit. Now they were widening the river and fortifying its stone walls, a much better idea. The two main streets leading to the hotel were both torn up, but we discovered this only after a tortuous (in a bus, anyway), twisting route through narrow alleys in pursuit of what looked like a detour but what was in fact a dead end.

We arrived at 8 P.M., exhausted, and still had to unload the bus. Alert storeroom girls at the hotel did us the service of counting our baggage: not counting the ones we took to our rooms, there were more than fifty pieces. And we would acquire still more in Kangding (a hundred kilos of vegetables, four people) and Derge (fifty kilos of potatoes, bedding, whisky, more people).

Waiting for us in the hotel lobby was a funny-looking, slightly built Chinese guy in a black suit, wearing glasses and with one tooth that stuck out of his mouth. He came straight up to me and said, in English, "Nyima Tsering sent me to meet you. My name is Wu. How can I help you?"

Here at last was heavenly intervention that brought me my much-needed interpreter. I said, "I need an interpreter for a month. What kind of wages do you want?"

He replied, "It doesn't matter. Whatever you want to pay."

I said, "You're hired."

Wu Bangfu, whose given name means "help to good fortune," came from a very poor farming district called Anyue in eastern Sichuan. He told me that even now, despite burgeoning prosperity in many parts of China, Anyue was still extremely poor, with no industry to speak of. He was the second of five children. He excelled in school, but because he was blind in one eye, no one thought he could go to college, for regulations limited precious university slots to healthy students. Nevertheless, Wu vowed to pass the college entrance examination, just to prove a point. On his first two tries he failed, due to poor health brought by undernourishment and too much study. Despite wavering parental support for this hopeless endeavor, he studied for one more year, took the test again, and passed with high marks. Then, to everyone's amazement, and despite regulations, he was admitted to Neijiang Teacher's College.

Mr. Wu was a physics major, but he taught himself English on the side. After graduation, he applied for a position as an English teacher in Kangding, where English treachers were in great demand. At that time, he had never been to Kangding and knew nothing of Tibetans. The roads were so bad it took four days to reach the town from Chengdu. In his adopted home he met his wife, who is Tibetan. They and their little girl were living in an apartment attached to the wife's work unit.

In the morning I marshaled my lieutenants, Mr. Wu and Denba Dargye, whom we just called Denba. They were joined by a new recruit, a man called Kunchok Dorje, who hailed from Derge and would be operating the video camera I had brought along. We laid out our areas of attack, in order of priority: find a bus,[64] locate our students, buy supplies, and turn in our paperwork to the prefectural foreign affairs office. It was a blessed relief to have competent lieutenants after years of doing it all myself. The only snag was over a prospective apprentice, a lad named Yama Tsering. He worked for the Ganzi Cultural Affairs Bureau, and when we innocently went to his boss to ask permission for a month's leave, we were admonished that we should have contacted this office years ago, at the very beginning of the program, for they have jurisdiction over preservation of cultural artifacts.[65] After we had wasted four hours duly kowtowing to these people, we were allowed to leave, but without Yama Tsering, who was needed in the office.

From Kangding, the road went on just as it always had, with perhaps a bit more pavement than previously, and a few more restaurants, microscopically cleaner. Progress was marching on, even out here. Having lost half a day in Kangding, we reached Trango at 3 P.M. on the second day— when we stopped to take Guido Botticelli to the hospital.

Guido was new. He was a white-haired bear of a man, bearded, 57 years old, gentle and kind. Carlo and Donatella had said that two conservators were not enough to accomplish the removal of two large walls

---

64 Chengdu drivers are usually unwilling to drive past Kangding into an area they consider primitive, alien, and dangerous. Kangding drivers and vehicles are much better suited to the terrain we were going into, thus all of my expeditions changed transport in Kangding.

65 Other government departments that were involved were the Religious Affairs Bureau, the Nationalities Affairs Bureau, the Foreign Affairs Bureau, the military, and Public Security. Many of these offices exist in triplicate: at county, prefecture, and provincial level. I also dealt with the governments of Derge County and Babang Township, the Derge Party Secretary, and of course the religious hierarchies of both monasteries, in residence and abroad. Any of these entities could have halted the program. Fortunately, none did.

of murals, and what could I do but agree? Not only that, but Guido was Italy's leading expert on detaching wall paintings. He was available and willing to come. So here he was.

Guido Botticelli.

During the three-day drive to Derge, Guido had been something of a running soap opera.[66] In Kangding, he had complained of headache and blood pressure. High or low? I wasn't sure; Guido couldn't speak English, and Donatella's translation was fuzzy. There, I had sent Mr. Wu to take Guido to the doctor, where he was given envelopes of reassuring pills.

At our first overnight stop, Guido suffered from headache and insomnia. The next day he was looking haggard. I was very worried, but the Trango doctor was clearly not impressed by the gravity of his condition. "There's nothing wrong with your heart. There's nothing wrong with you at all," she said scornfully in Chinese. Neither Mr. Wu nor I both-

66 It was subsequently suggested to me by Karen Yager (who appears in Chapter 14) that Guido's problems were perhaps caused by fumes from the ammonia we were carrying in the back of the bus. In Kangding we moved all the chemicals to the bus roof, but for Guido their effects apparently lingered.

ered to translate. Guido's blood pressure came out normal. When I asked about headache medicine, the doctor patiently wrote out a prescription for three different things (one was vitamins) that cost a grand total of 4.8 yuan, or sixty cents American. We got an oxygen bag for Tro La. We certainly looked grand parading down the streets of Trango with the big rubber oxygen pillow. At least the pills, oxygen, and attention all had a good effect on Guido's morale.

The next day, Guido survived Tro La very well, and we rolled into Derge at about 5 P.M. Apart from a bit of new construction, it was unchanged. Looking around the street at the disreputable characters with their lank hair and staring peasant eyes, it was hard to believe that Derge was the cultural center of anywhere. But so it is: the Khampa heartland, a repository for art and history, a training ground for craftsmen, and the site of the Derge Printing House and all its literary treasures.

Shongshong and Tenzeng Nyima were waiting on the street. We learned that Pewar Rinpoche was expected, having departed from Kangding this morning along with another tulku, a visiting exile, who would conduct a month of teachings here. Although the two could not possibly arrive for another twenty hours, several dozen Tibetans, mostly elderly, were already lined up by the roadside to greet the revered travelers.

Shongshong had good news: he had already booked our truck and horses for the morning.

The next day, an open truck and a battered police car took ourselves and our baggage to the trailhead. We found waiting for us there two villages' worth of horses—about thirty—together with twenty-five wranglers. Everyone got busy pulling bags and boxes from the truck and heaping them on the ground. The gear made an alarmingly large pile. All thirteen team members milled around.[67] I started sweating. How would it all fit? Clever Denba led the experts to a meadow and laid out a picnic for them. Clearly, it would be a while before we could hit the trail.

---

67 Myself and three Italian experts, Denba, Mr. Wu, video cameraman Kunchok Dorje, a policeman named Buge, Yangjin and another student from Kangding, Shongshong, Tenzeng Nyima, and a carpenter named Tashi Dendrup.

I stayed behind, pulling out bags labeled "Very Important" and sorting them into a separate pile. The wranglers swarmed over everything. They looked dismayed. We had two villages, so their first order of business was to split the goods between them. They completely dismantled my two piles, then set about creating two new piles carefully balanced by weight. This involved splitting all pairs of well-matched bags that would have gone very well on the opposite sides of a horse. The men shouted and haggled all at once, while the horses stood by, jingling their bells and ripping up mouthfuls of grass.

When the split was accomplished, with great ceremony the two headmen drew straws to see which village would get which pile. After that, the arguments were over and they got down to the business of loading their now rigorously mismatched bags onto the horses. Many of the bags had to be opened and their contents distributed among other bags. A lot of cans, noodles, and other food items that had been painstakingly packed were emptied into leather packsacks. The fiberglass roll was completely unrolled and divided into component sheets.

Rural Tibetans treat all kinds of luggage the same way: like a sack of grain. They stack it any old way, throw it when it needs to be somewhere else, kick it when they want to see how soft or hard it is, and show utter disdain for corners, remaking the shape to match the interior of a saddlebag by sheer brute force. I had labored long and hard to educate my staff in the art of packing. Still, many boxes had holes and tears after four days in the back of a bus. Now they were abused even more. All I could do was stand back with a weary smile and hope that the conservators would stay in their meadow around the bend and not come to witness the savagery being done to their equipment. Tubs of solvent were turned upside down. Boxes were ripped open. The only thing that seemed immune to damage were the packages of Cheetos and milk powder, which had expanded under the difference in air pressure and were now like little balloons.

After a couple of hours, most of the team had been assigned their mounts and had ridden ahead. Only when I saw the final few bags going onto the final horse, did I dare to turn my face toward the trail. It was a difficult ride, because the county had begun opening a motorable road that would eventually go all the way to Palpung. The old trail was torn up, and we had to dismount many times so the horses could be led. Loads slid off and snagged on rocks and trees. It began to rain.

We reached Pewar at dusk. Unloading was a scene of incredible confusion; wet people, horses, and bags swamped the courtyard. Later, an inventory showed that the only things missing were scalpels and some spices whose loss was the cause of much despair, as a month of chili- and MSG-less meals is enough to dishearten any Sichuan person, Tibetan or not. A week or so later, however, both were found among our bags.

CHAPTER 12

IN A STORY told in Pewar's murals, a man stands in a cauldron of fire, his face stretched in agony.

Once, at Gaya, The Awakened One preached a Fire Sermon, saying:

"Monks, the All is aflame. What All is aflame? The eye is aflame. Forms are aflame. Aflame with what? Aflame with the fire of passion, the fire of aversion, the fire of delusion. Aflame, I tell you, with birth, aging & death, with sorrows, lamentations, pains, distresses & despairs.

"The ear is aflame. Sounds are aflame . . .

"The nose is aflame. Aromas are aflame . . .

"The tongue is aflame. Flavors are aflame . . .

"The body is aflame. Tactile sensations are aflame . . .

"The intellect is aflame. Ideas are aflame.

"Seeing thus, the instructed noble disciple grows disenchanted with the eye, disenchanted with forms, disenchanted with consciousness at the eye, disenchanted with contact at the eye. And whatever there is that arises in dependence on contact at the eye, experienced as pleasure, pain or neither pleasure-nor-pain: With that, too, he grows disenchanted.

"He grows disenchanted with the ear . . .

"He grows disenchanted with the nose . . .

"He grows disenchanted with the tongue . . .

"He grows disenchanted with the body . . .

"He grows disenchanted with the intellect, disenchanted with ideas. Disenchanted, he becomes dispassionate. Through dispassion, he is fully released."

In Pewar's painting, the burning man reaches out, out of the flames. He grasps the hand of a monk, ready to pull him free. In taking refuge, then, the fires of samsara are quenched.

May 5

Today, I had a reminder of how hard it is to detach a painting: the first test failed. When they peeled the mural from the wall, some color was left behind. Fortunately, the tests were being performed on the lousy recent paintings, not on the original ancient murals, so there was no great loss. But the failure, if it could not be remedied, would make it impossible to do the job for which we had come.

I asked Donatella, "What is the problem?"

"It might be the fixative," she said carefully. "Or maybe the glue is not enough strong," She refrained from accusations. But if it was the glue, I knew it was my fault.

Here's what had happened. In 1995, when they performed the first detachment test, she and Carlo had used animal glue and other materials brought from Italy. They had brought only small amounts, but still the excess baggage charges on their airfare to Chengdu had been atrocious. This year, I was determined to find a source of materials somewhere closer. After some detective work, I found a dealer, National Starch and Chemical, in Hong Kong. From them I obtained a sample of animal glue called K-38, which I express-mailed to Guido in Florence. He tested it and pronounced it suitable.

When I went back to make the purchase, however, the company told me that they were out of K-38; how would I like some K-36? It's the same thing, really, they said. There was no time to send the K-36 to Italy for testing. The company could provide no solid data on the properties of the two glues—not that I had any idea what to look for. I must have called the salesman half a dozen times, until they started telling me that he was not in the office. For a sale worth less than U.S.$100 to them, my questions just weren't worth their trouble.

Now it seemed that my bothersome questions were crucial to the mission's success.

Two days went by and they had two more unsuccessful tests. The cause was definitely the K-36 glue I bought in Hong Kong. So not only might the mission fail, but it would be my fault for not telling the conservators to bring their own glue from Italy after the company switched products on me. I carried on as usual. But my heart was heavy with worry.

The weather had been relentlessly cold, cloudy, and damp—a far cry from the heavenly conditions we enjoyed the previous year. The wind blew up a storm, and hail fell on the monastery. It was a sobering reminder of the relentless environment of Tibet's high plateau.

There was one ray of hope: Guido. He had been detaching wall paintings for thirty years. Perhaps he could think of a way out.

He did. At the conclusion of the next test, instead of peeling the painting off the wall, he used a mallet and pounded it, turning the clay underneath to dust. I was amazed that he could do this without damaging the painting, but that's what his thirty years of experience was good for. The separation now occurred inside the clay instead of inside the pigment. It was a very labor-intensive process. But, by God, it worked.

Detaching the painting was, however, only half the job. The other half was to prepare the painting to be remounted. To do this, they would apply a new backing on the painting, then remove gauze and K-36 glue from the front. Donatella told me that if plastificants such as formaldehyde had been added to the K-36, then it wouldn't solve, and they would be unable to remove the facing. It would do no good to save paintings if they would be forever encased in a glue-and-gauze bandage. Were there plastificants in K-36? The literature faxed by National Starch and Chemical didn't mention any. But my phone calls to Hong Kong to confirm this point had never been returned, a fact that no one knew but me. Now, all I could do was live with the gnawing nightmare anxiety that our mission would fail after all, just because of my stupid carelessness.

The next morning I awoke to rain—highly inauspicious—and a sinking feeling that this would be a bad, bad day.

The team, however, had no idea of the heaviness in my heart. They brought the test section of mural into the common room, where it was laid out on a makeshift table of boards. The cooks had been instructed to get a fire going ahead of time and to boil a large kettle of water. The three conservators gathered their tools and briefed their helpers. Like an open-heart surgery patient, the painting on the table was surrounded by busy workers. Around them, everyone in the monastery had come to watch the miracle unfold.

Removing gauze from the front of a mural.

First, the conservators laid a piece of hot, damp felt on the painting. To keep it hot, they covered it with plastic bags full of more hot water. The bags were allowed to sit for about twenty minutes so that the gauze and animal glue was thoroughly steamed. (The backing was held by a different glue, insoluble in water, so it would not come off during this process.)

After a time they removed the bags and felt. They dribbled more hot water onto the now-sticky gauze, sponged the water up carefully, gradually soaking up the glue. Apprentices cleaned the sponges, and kept them ready to hand like surgical instruments. Water carriers leaped to respond to Donatella's repeated cries of *"acqua! acqua!"* for the water kept going cold. Sponges flew from hand to hand. After a time, the gauze was no longer yellow-tinted, so they stopped sponging the mural. Slowly and carefully, Guido began to peel up gauze from the painting's surface.

No plasticants. Whew!

As the first layer of gauze came off, a painted figure started to emerge like a shapely nude in a steamy shower. After they removed the second layer of gauze, a warm, wet, profoundly delicate canvas-backed painting lay limply on the table. The conservators sponged the painting carefully to soak up remaining glue, and I was disturbed to see some color coming up, especially the blue, which was particularly weak.

Over the next couple of days they tinkered with the fixative, to see if they could solve the problem. Fixative is painted onto the mural to protect the color before gauze is applied. We had two kinds: paraloid and vinavil (Elmer's glue), although not enough of the former to do the entire job. Donatella said, "To carry all the materials that you might need to this remote place is really impossible. So you have to adjust everything, because you don't have enough of anything." It was a problem we would face again and again. Each time the experts ran short of materials, or conditions such as lighting, temperature, and ventilation weren't right, or tools were broken, they put their heads together and devised a way around the problem. I had imagined that detaching murals was a cookbook process, but now I saw that it requires constant adaptation.

The additional tests were not successful, so the conservators decided to stay with the original technique. We would lose some blue pigment, but it was better than losing the entire mural.

Yangjin continued to be our star apprentice, the favorite of Guido and the other experts. We had brought a new monk apprentice from Kangding, but he was hopeless. I wrote in my diary, "Poor Gonga! He is just not suited for this work, doesn't understand anything, and the Italians keep yelling at him. Maybe I should send him home—but at the cost of so much face!" Fang, the Chinese student from last year, had moved out of the prefecture and could not come. Aga had promised to join us but had not yet appeared. In his absence, we had conscripted a young Pewar monk called Trajia and a carpenter named Tashi Dendrup, who also worked for us making tables, scaffolding, and mallets. The three were smart, hard working, and careful, but not even Yangjin fulfilled all the qualifications of a full-fledged conservation student, for she lacked the chemistry training and language skills that she would need if she were ever admitted to an institute abroad.

I had to admit that our plan for training Tibetans as conservators was a little too ambitious. In China, college-bound Tibetans usually lack preparation to become chemistry or English majors; instead they are steered toward "nationality institutes" where they end up studying ethnology or some other social science. Regardless of nationality, the average college graduate in China isn't interested in traipsing around to remote, uncomfortable monasteries; he or she is looking to land a cushy desk job. It will take at least another generation before Tibetans will flock to art conservation like Italians do now. By that time, there may be nothing left to conserve.

Now that they had worked out the method of detachment, the conservators were gearing up for full-scale removal of the major mural sections on the south and east walls. Meanwhile, I had a cold that just wouldn't quit. It had started on road and had hung on doggedly ever since. But nobody, including me, paid it much attention. I had business at Palpung, and after that I wanted to explore some new territory. Shong-shong, the cameraman Kunchok Dorje, and Denba would accompany me. Tenzeng Nyima found horses for us, and after a couple of days we hit the trail, heading upriver.

May 10

Palpung was changed, joyously so! No longer was it a hollow, haunted mansion. As we climbed the staircase to our quarters, we met cavalcades of workers, baskets in hand. Sawhorses and stacks of freshly milled timber blocked the corridors, and wood chips perfumed the air. On the roof, a gang of women were singing as they spread clay. Best of all, atop the highest part of the temple, was a gleaming gold beacon, a *sedong* (steeple). It was a symbol of Palpung's rebirth, for during the Cultural Revolution the building had been stripped of all that was precious.

---

68 Jamgön Kongtrül Rinpoche is one of the four incarnate lamas who traditionally make Palpung their seat. The individual who donated the *sedong* was living in exile in India, where he attended upon the Karmapa, leader of the Karma Kagyu lineage. He also was highly regarded

"Five years ago," Shongshong explained, "Kongtrül Rinpoche[68] pledged to replace Palpung's *sedong*. Even though he died in a car crash in 1992, his followers kept the promise. It came from India. It's got 3.8 *jin*[69] of gold on it, applied in Lhasa before it was shipped here." I tried to imagine the *sedong* coming to Palpung. The thing was man-high at least, perhaps two meters around, and composed of hammered sheet metal—surely very heavy. How did they lug it over the passes? Not to worry: Where Buddhism is concerned, Tibetans have no end of ingenuity.

As I walked around Palpung, memories came welling up out of the woodwork: Here's where John Sanday lectured the monks, here are Urgyen Rinpoche's quarters, there's where dogs chomped my leg, here's where I lay while Aga cleaned my wounds. The spaces were the same, but so much was transformed! Situ Rinpoche had sent 25,000 yuan the previous year, so Shongshong was replacing, it seemed, half the building. Everywhere, new timber fit neatly around chocolate-colored old beams. Shongshong showed me an old discarded piece: it looked fine on the outside, but the inside was so tunneled through with termite trails that I could break it in my hands.

My feelings were all mixed up: gladness for the change, surprise that it came without my hearing, sadness for the old pieces thrown away, worry that the facelift wouldn't solve Palpung's deep structural ills, regret that we were not behind it—but wait a minute, yes we were, for we gave them money for some of this new wood.

Shongshong was unstoppable, and soon he would be wrecking a similar transformation at Pewar. Our whole plan—to preserve the old timber instead of replacing it—was in tatters, but it seemed that Shongshong was right after all. Or was he? Could John Sanday have saved some of this wood?

I felt guilty that we gave only dribs and drabs of help to Palpung while we undertook a major project down river at Pewar. I came expecting

as a teacher in his own right, with a large international following. He returned to Palpung in 1984 and 1991 to conduct empowerments there. The other three tulkus who traditionally reside at Palpung are Tai Situ Rinpoche, Khyentse Rinpoche, and Urgyen Rinpoche. Only the last is currently in residence.

69 A *jin* is half a kilogram.

reproach from the monks, but they had nothing of the kind: only a welcoming silk scarf and a hot dinner.

Timbers freshly replaced on the north wall of Palpung's main courtyard.

Workers stamp on clay to make a rammed earth wall for Palpung's new College of Buddhism, which lies above the main monastery. Situ Rinpoche donated the funds for construction.

Three days quickly sped by, but I wasn't going back to Pewar yet. I was going to another, more distant monastery called Dzongsar.

May 12   ୬୨୨

We set out for the seven-hour ride to Dzongsar with horses, wranglers, and a saddlebag full of provisions. Denba had passed on this side trip, preferring to return to the creature comforts of our base camp at Pewar. Now with just Shongshong and Kunchok Dorje, both Derge men, I was traveling the Tibetan way: lightly, my only concessions to foreign comforts a few toiletries, a journal, camera, and sleeping bag. Our guide carried the all-important tea kettle. As we climbed to the 4350-meter (14,272 feet) Ha La, the sun came out for the first time in days. I doffed a couple of layers and contemplated happy visions of glue drying speedily on Pewar's murals.

We stopped at noon on a great pasture, unloaded the horses and turned them loose to graze. Lunch was tea boiled over a campfire, dough fritters from a sack, and dried yak.

Mesho (Maisu in Chinese), the place we reached in late afternoon, teeters on the semantic divide between a village and a town. It was a marvelous conglomeration of Derge-style log houses along a river by the same name. Children came to greet me with flowers. A dirt road wound alongside the river, but I saw no motorized traffic on it. Compared to Palpung, Mesho was low, warm, and clean—a little paradise.

From Mesho, there was a not inconsiderable climb to the kingly complex of Dzongsar Monastery, overlooking the riverside settlement from a high bluff. Dzongsar's walls were striped in red, white, and black, emblematic of the Sakya order.[70]

Dzongsar Gonpa was founded in the thirteenth century. The name means "new fortress," the old fortress having been located on a neighboring ridge, its remnants all but vanished. Inhabitants say that the valley at one time belonged to the clan of King Gesar, but some 400 years ago

---

70 Derge county has a total of fifty-seven active monasteries divided among the five orders as follows: eighteen Sakya, fourteen Nyingma, eleven Kagyu, ten Bön, and four Gelug.

it was conquered by the Derge King and added to his domain. Dzongsar was completely destroyed in 1959 during a political witch hunt that accompanied the toppling of Communist Party figure Liu Shaoqi. Much of Dzongsar has since been rebuilt, and more work is ongoing.[71]

Dzongsar Monastery.

We were escorted into a large four-story building. Quarters for incarnate lamas were on the upper floors, guest rooms in the basement. Naked timber was everywhere; the furniture was minimally painted, and thankas and banners hung sparingly. It felt clean, solid, and well-built, but utterly lacked the august patina that distinguishes Palpung.

Below Dzongsar is a *shedra* (Buddhist college) on the valley floor. Founded in the nineteenth century, it teaches an eclectic fusion of Nyingma, Sakya, and Kagyu traditions. Of the perhaps dozen *shedra* presently operating in Ganzi Prefecture, the school at Dzongsar is widely held to

71 Appendix IV gives details of the destruction and reconstruction of Dzongsar and some other monasteries in Ganzi Prefecture.

be the best. It currently has 150 students and offers programs in painting, carving, and medicine, as well as philosophy.

Shongshong, the cameraman Kunchok Dorje, and I settled into our various lodgings. Respectively, we three had come for the not very defensible reasons of blessings, footage, and new terrain. On the first day, I attended an empowerment ceremony officiated by Khyentse Norbu Rinpoche,[72] a visiting exile who had attracted a huge number of pilgrims.

Like other attendees, who were nearly all monks, all day long I sat cross-legged on the cold temple floor having holy water splashed on me at intervals. By sunset, I was shaking and feverish. The next morning I was too ill to eat or even get out of bed; but we had work to do at Pewar, so, on the third day, seeing that I was somewhat better, Shongshong and Kunchok Dorje propped me up on a horse and brought me home.

At Pewar, it wasn't long before three more victims were felled by what we christened the "Palpung Virus." We had no doctor, so Yangjin took charge of the medical kit, handing out pills and using our disposable needles to inject penicillin into the sufferers.[73] Fortunately, none of the Italian experts caught the bug (which would have set the work back seriously), and after a week or so everyone recovered.

I had returned to Pewar just in time to watch them take down the last section of mural. The conservators and their students were a smoothly functioning team by now, and not even the inept Gonga needed to be told what to do. As they beat the painting with wooden mallets, I gave a sidelong glance at Tenzeng Nyima, who had been with us at Dzongsar and was therefore seeing this procedure for the first time. Luckily, he didn't seem overly concerned about the ecclesiastical implications of pounding on deities.

Bang, bang, bang went the mallets. Dust flew, clay crumbled, and soon the mural was hanging free from the wall like a curtain. Carlo, Guido, and Gonga rolled up the mural and carried it to another room

72 He is perhaps best known to the West for his work as advisor to Bernardo Bertolucci for the film "Little Buddha." He subsequently wrote and directed "The Cup," the world's first Tibetan-language feature film.

73 Doctors in China have been using penicillin to treat influenza for years, and people have unshakeable faith in its efficacy.

where excess clay was scraped from the back by Donatella and Yangjin. Then the mural was stored, along with the others, in a room of the monastery. Apart from the one section that had been unfaced already, the murals would keep their facings until we could come back. Meanwhile, the walls and roof of Pewar's lantern would be rebuilt.

The work completed, we packed up and went back to Derge.

That's where all hell broke loose.

CHAPTER 13

As you enter Pewar's main temple, peering over your left shoulder are the three glaring eyes of *Gurgyi Gonpo*. This fierce, bare-fanged, snarling apparition is called the Great Vajra Black One, Lord of the Canopy. He is a wrathful deity, an archetypal image of primordial energy. A potbellied creature, Gurgyi Gonpo is black-skinned and splay-legged; he wears a crown of five skulls, on his necklace hang fifty freshly severed heads, and he tramples on a corpse.

To the dharma practitioner, the deity's appearance is not meant to frighten; instead, it signifies ferocity in the war against delusion. The pool of flames that surrounds him represents pristine awareness. The gruesome trophies represent defeated passions. The curved knife in his right hand and skullcap in his left are for cutting off defilements.

May 21

Malu had been unable to come this time, and so our police escort was another fellow, a portly Derge native named Buge, bullheaded and not very bright. He had been with us last year and distinguished himself by performing not one single useful function—not even minding the security of our stores or keeping riff-raff away. (I was afraid that if the wrong people saw the detachment process, it might be used to steal paintings for the black market.) What Buge mainly did was sit around the common room smoking and chatting with other less-than-fully-occupied team members such as Denba. That, and eat.

Of course, Buge was not there at my invitation; he was sent to be the government's eyes and ears, and to enforce the law. Out of all the outlaw possibilities, we had only one illegal thing on our minds: photographing the murals. But this was enough to provoke Buge to become my personal nemesis.

Yes, it's true: somewhere in the great labyrinth of Chinese regulations there is one prohibiting foreigners from photographing temple interiors. I don't know the reason for this, but I guess that it's one or more of the following: (1) to minimize damage by flashbulbs; (2) to ensure proper respect for sacred sites; (3) to prevent foreigners from reaping profits on China's cultural artifacts. However, the fact is that at many famous sites such as Jokhang Temple in Lhasa, one can buy a photography permit from the monks. (That was the situation in 1993; by 1997 the Jokhang monks had given up, and Tibet's most sacred temple was a free-for-all.)

Buge did not know the reason for the rule either. He didn't need to know, because it was not his job to think. His job was enforcement. He did decide that photography of the upper murals, the ones we were detaching, was permitted. I argued that we were saving the lower murals as well, and that photography was a necessary part of the conservation process, and that furthermore I needed pictures in order to raise money for the program, for what sponsor in his right mind is going to give money to save murals he can't see?

Buge wasn't having any of this, but I continued to press him, so eventually he decreed that I could photograph every other panel. "This one, and that one, and that one . . .," he said, pointing at images on the wall. I figured I'd better work fast before he changed his mind. I set up my camera, and under his watchful eyes proceeded to photograph the indicated murals until I came to one blocked by a large altar. To move the altar out of the way would have been a lot of effort, so I unilaterally decided to swap it for a neighbor, a painting Buge hadn't chosen.

At this, Buge decided that I had gone too far. He didn't say anything then, but by the time we returned to Derge he had evidently decided that the situation was simply too dangerous for him, and he'd better cover his rear. So he went to the police chief and reported the whole business, apparently not mentioning having ever given permission for anything.

So here I was, fresh from the triumph of a successful mission, sitting in the police chief's office trying to sort out this mess. The man was Chinese, new on the job, neither helpful like Malu nor someone capable of creative decision making. He asked for my film. First he wanted just the mural pictures, then he said he wanted all of it, of whatever subject, including the video that Kunchok Dorje had shot. The contraband articles would be shipped to Kangding. There, some higher authority would look at them and decide if I should have them back.

Confident that I would be exonerated in the end, I gave him about ten cans, randomly selected, and three out of the four videocassettes, hiding the remainder. No one in Derge or Kangding could develop slide film, and no one but I had a machine compatible with the tapes, but the police chief was not interested in these technical details. He wanted to pass the buck to his superior.

Here, Mr. Wu pulled a rabbit out of his hat. He proposed we go to see the county Party Secretary, who happened to be his wife's relative. The gentleman, who was named Qing Gang, was working late in his office when we went there at the eleventh hour to beg for intervention. I had never been in an office of a Party Secretary before, and goggled a bit at the huge desk, heavy red velvet curtains, and enormous Mao portrait on the wall. Mr. Qing was fiftyish, short and stout, with a receding hairline and long combed-back hair that gave him a nauseating resemblance to the Great Helmsman.

Wu explained the whole sordid affair, while Qing listened, looking displeased. He asked a few questions, and they conversed in rapid Sichuan-*hua*. I did not have a good feeling. Qing picked up his telephone and got somebody on the line. "He's calling the police chief," Mr. Wu whispered.

Qing issued some curt commands into the telephone, listened to the reply, then signed off and put down the receiver. "What happened?" I asked Wu. After some communication between the two relations, Mr. Wu said, "Mr. Qing Gang asked the police chief to give you back your film, but the police chief said it's too late. The matter has already been reported to Kangding. Mr. Qing Gang cannot go against the prefectural police."

This silly business was becoming a federal case!

Now I knew there was no hope. I headed back to the police station with a last-ditch proposal that Denba or someone else in my party could act as courier for the film, so it wouldn't get lost on the way to Kangding. But as Wu and I approached the station, we saw a huge crowd milling in front. "Find out what's going on," I said to Mr. Wu.

Minutes later he came back to report that a murderer had just been captured and brought in. Although homicide is not rare in Kham—warrior traditions still run strong—killers are rarely caught. This was therefore a signal event in a small town like Derge. Mr. Wu learned that the killer had stabbed another man and a three-year-old baby in a blood feud, not far away in the township of Changra. He had been injured in the course of being apprehended, and was now in the hospital under guard.

There was no way anyone in Derge was going to give a damn about my film now. I threw in the towel and went to bed. We left early the next morning.

The mission was over, and now, back in Hong Kong and Los Angeles, the really hard work would resume: fundraising. Pewar's murals were safely rolled up and stored in the monastery. All except one panel still had gauze facing attached. Donatella said we would have to go back and finish the job within two years, or else the paintings wouldn't be recoverable. That meant another expedition costing a minimum of $40,000—assuming that I continued to be unpaid, and the conservators would still agree to take half their usual salary. Plus, Shongshong would need money to replace the damaged walls and roof.

Shongshong planned that in late autumn he would cover the lower murals with a protective layer of cotton, fabric, and timber. In early winter he would tear down the old roof of Pewar, and the upstairs lantern with its now-naked walls. Then everyone would pray for dry, stable weather while workmen quickly put up a new roof. Winter is the driest season on the Tibetan plateau; nevertheless, for several weeks the temple would be open to the sky and whatever nastiness it might dish out. It would be a white-knuckle operation. I had to make sure Shongshong didn't run out of money in the middle.

In my quest to find money for Pewar and Palpung, I had left few stones unturned. The Getty Grant Program, initiator of the project and supporter of art conservation efforts around the world, responded to my letter of inquiry by saying they would not invite a proposal. I spent a week crafting a proposal for a Japanese organization, but they didn't even acknowledge receiving it. I sent a proposal to Richard Gere's foundation in New York, but they neither replied nor returned my phone calls.

Meanwhile, I worked on publicity. I lectured relentlessly in Hong Kong and California, and wrote articles for magazines. From the single unconfiscated videotape, CNN International constructed a six-minute segment that aired around the world. An outfit called Asian Arts in Santa Fe created and hosted an elaborate site on the World Wide Web for the project. My book, *Among Warriors*, bought me a bit of recognition in the community of people who care about Tibet. Gradually, the work at Pewar became known.

Between 1994 and 1998, out of this mountain of effort, came a few successes. A privately managed trust sent two donations of about $25,000 each in successive years. Wong How Man, who was peerless when it came to fund-raising among Chinese businessmen, located a charity in Taiwan that contributed $25,000. The Durfee Foundation—the same people who had sent me on my original Kham wanderings back in 1991—pledged three years of support at $20,000 per year starting in 1997. We got several $5000 donations from Art Restoration for Cultural Heritage, an Austrian nonprofit run by Francesca van Habsburg.

Between Wong How Man and myself, we found enough cash—always at the last minute—for each mission to keep the program going. It was a shoestring budget for a complicated art conservation effort like the one we were running at Pewar. For Palpung, there was nothing at all—unless I could think of something.

The problem was that I was part of the China Exploration and Research Society. This organization is, very reasonably, based in Hong Kong, where it benefits from the personal magnetism of Wong How Man, who enjoys a huge and flamboyant reputation as the colony's foremost native-born explorer. Most of CERS's sponsors were corporations with Hong Kong offices and major investments in the mainland. They were happy to support Wong's projects in other parts of China, but the word "Tibet" was a red light. People just wouldn't believe that the Chinese government had sanctioned our work in Derge. The companies feared any association with the Dalai Lama might hurt their businesses. So they all said no.

Meanwhile, the U.S. economy was strong, and American interest in Tibet was high. I had always believed that if people could just see Pewar and Palpung, they would want to help. So I created an organization of my own, called the Kham Aid Foundation, based in Los Angeles. Two friends came in with me, joining the board of directors of the fledging nonprofit, which would have 501(c)(3) status and could therefore offer that all-important tax deduction to U.S. donors. As president of an American organization, I could be a credible grant writer to potential U.S. funders. Wong How Man supported this move, even assenting to my proposal that program management gradually be taken over by my U.S. office. The work in Derge had been growing ever more expensive, complex, and burdensome. He was pleased to be relieved of it.

My first project with Kham Aid Foundation was to organize a tour to Derge, the profits of which would go to saving Pewar and Palpung. I thought my tour would be attractive to those who want their trip to make a real difference for Tibetans, not just add to a travel outfitter's bottom line. I was right, for my modest advertising campaign led to eleven sign-ups for the first tour, which was scheduled for September 1997.

Then, in August, as I was finalizing tour arrangements, something happened that turned my plans upside down. A U.S. congressman, Frank Wolf, went to Tibet without permission or knowledge of the Chinese government. He returned to Washington and called a press conference in which he delivered a sensational account of the "unspeakably brutal conditions" in Tibet.

Beijing was infuriated and branded the incident as espionage. The Sichuan government came down with a ban on all travel in Tibetan areas by Americans. When the news reached me that our travel permits had been denied, I was already in Chengdu, my clients only days from arriving.

My back was against the wall. If I called the tour off, the clients would be stuck with nonreturnable air tickets and no Tibet trip. To change the itinerary to a completely different route—Chamdo to Lhasa—seemed the lesser of two evils. Oddly enough, it was not difficult to procure permits for these areas, as the ruling troika of police, military, and foreign affairs reacted to the incident with less severity in the Tibet Autonomous Region than in Sichuan—this despite truckloads of riot police tooling around Lhasa in full view of foreign tourists. I informed the clients by e-mail of the change. A few days later they arrived, ready if not entirely willing to wing it.

Disaster followed upon disaster. We couldn't fly to Chamdo as planned because of bad weather, so cars and staff who had been sent there were abandoned while we flew to Lhasa instead at major added cost. After a couple of days of sightseeing in Lhasa, the local company who was organizing our trip sent us to Tsurphu Monastery. There, two clients fell ill from altitude sickness, one of them seriously enough to go home. Food was inadequate, and everyone was hungry. The drivers were incompetent; cars were in bad condition. Clients begged me to take them back to Lhasa, where they could eat nice food and stay in rooms with hot water—the cost of which would come straight out of money I wanted for Palpung. With each pass through Lhasa, people disappeared, some demanding refunds on their way out.

Others, I was thankful to see, stuck with me, and after I learned how to ride herd on the stingy tour company, things went more smoothly. We saw some amazing sights: Lake Nam Tso, a sacred hot spring, a sky burial. I had guessed right: that bringing people to Tibet would inspire them to get involved, but their involvement was with Lhasa and its environs, not with Kham. The $5000 earned by the tour for Kham Aid Foundation was a poor harvest for a month of my time and so much aggravation.

When the ordeal of the tour was over, I flew back to Chengdu. Shongshong and Tenzeng Nyima came down from Derge to meet me. Shongshong, I noticed, had traded his Tibetan robe for a plain dark overcoat, the better to fit into the teaming city. He and Tenzeng Nyima seemed to be navigating Chengdu successfully, purchasing cement and other items that would be shipped back to Derge. We went over the expenses of previous months.

Among Tenzeng Nyima's receipts was an unusual item: 2325 yuan for "transportation of injured workers." There had been an accident, Shongshong explained, involving villagers from across the Dri Chu who had volunteered to help with the construction. They were being carried to Pewar on the monastery's tractor, when the tractor overturned on a steep slope. Three people were injured, including the driver, and one elderly woman was killed on the spot.

Shongshong immediately contacted Pewar Rinpoche. He came at once, making the long trip from Chengdu to Pewar in March, one of the worst seasons for travel. He visited the bereaved family several times, offered prayers for the dead woman and presented her family with a cow among other gifts. They pronounced themselves satisfied, and willingly applied their thumbprints to a letter stating so. Shongshong explained the whole thing to me very straightforwardly, saying, "I've got to tell you the bad news as well as the good," as he showed me the letter.

I was shocked by the news that someone had died saving Pewar, but as the matter had already been worked out to everyone's satisfaction, there was nothing for me to do.

A day or two later, Shongshong and Tenzeng Nyima left Chengdu, heading for the sacred mountain Emei Shan, where they would undertake a pilgrimage. It gave me pleasure to think of the two inseparable Tibetans climbing Emei's endless steps along with hordes of doughty Chinese grandmas. Feeling somewhat more optimistic, I headed back to Los Angeles.

By now, the adventure value of this project was starting to wear thin. During stints of fund-raising at home, I lived on money left to me by my father, which was sufficient for my needs but a distinct step down from my former salary as a Ph.D. scientist. More important, boyfriends vanished during these trips to Tibet, and friends seemed to forget my telephone number. I was once proud that I could live contentedly without hot running water, supermarkets, freeways, and television; but by now, after these expeditions, I was joyfully embracing them. Nevertheless, I had no thought of quitting.

In the spring of 1998, Shongshong sent word that he had changed

Pewar's roof without mishap, and built new walls for the murals. The money situation wasn't great, nor was my morale; but this was no time to falter. The stage was set for our last—and most critical—mission.

Fifth Mission: 1998

〜〜

CHAPTER 14

SARASVATI, the Hindu goddess of music, poetry, and wisdom, sits to Gurgyi Gonpo's left. Her legs are crossed, with feet on the floor; she plucks at a lute that she carries in her arms.

Sarasvati found an earthly emanation in Yeshe Tsogyal—"Ocean of Unending Primordial Wisdom." A woman of divine beauty and towering intellect, Yeshi Tsogyal became Tibet's greatest female philosopher. In 772, she was given by king Trisong Detsen to the great Indian sage Padmasambhava. Under pressure from anti-Buddhist forces in court, the two fled to the mountains. Together, the couple practiced meditation in a cave at Tidrom, a site now hallowed as a source of feminine power and sublime inspiration. When her guru was absent, she undertook long pilgrimages, and spent three years practicing austerities in a snowy retreat.

With her perfect recall, Yeshi Tsogyal was able to remember, record, and codify Padmasambhava's teachings; she also wrote many learned commentaries of her own. These written treasures she secreted around Tibet, intending, in the ripeness of time, that they be discovered by future disciples.

April 6, Tawu County 〜〜

KABLOOOOOM! That was the sound of the first wrinkle in an otherwise flawless mission, a trip that was uncannily smooth until this moment. It was a loud explosion, very close, but what the heck was it? Dust is flying around inside the bus. The truck just ahead of us slowed down, too, as if they thought it was *their* vehicle that had exploded. The bus bobbles to a halt; driver gets out, walks backward. I lean out of my window to look back, and see a loose flap of bus hanging in the breeze, as if a grenade went off inside. The team is buzzing with confusion, excitement, even laughter (it's that kind of group).

Expedition bus interior, on the road.

The bus door opens, so I climb over baggage to the outside, walk around to where some of the more alert team members (read: nonforeigners) are gathering around, pointing. There is a GIGANTIC rip in the tire, and the wheel well surrounding it has been blackened and pushed away. Inside the bus, the floor is about six inches higher than it was previously. Karen Yager, who was sitting on top of the explosion, has an injured ankle and somehow twisted her glasses. She is laughing. They are all laughing. It's that kind of trip.

Female team members fan out into the bushes, looking for places to pee. The driver and assorted unskilled helpers change the tire, and I revise our goals for today. We will not make it to Trango. We will go to Tawu, just 30 kilometers ahead, and repair this mess. We need a new tire, and the bus has to be welded back together. The apprentices lean on a giant lug wrench to fasten the spare. They tape the flap closed and lay plastic bags on the floor to keep out the dust.

As we drive away, Karen has abandoned her damaged seat and come forward to sit with me, raising her injured ankle on the bench in front.

Peng Jing and the expedition bus.

"The funny thing is," she says, "that the road for the last few miles has been fairly flat: no big stones or anything." I mentally speculate on the pressure-temperature time history of the air inside our tires. She is dangling pieces of equipment: video battery pack, still camera, video recorder, tape cases, and bag, all of which she trailed behind her when she changed her seat. Cameraman Chimei Dorje gallantly stows her bag and compresses some of her dangles. It's getting dark.

I was so dreading this mission; knew it would be a complicated one; knew time would be very tight; but lo and behold I must be getting good at this because it's gone more smoothly than any trip I've led, ever. Flying in just five days before launch was crazy, but I got away with it. I picked up Kel during a one-hour layover in Hong Kong, brought us to Chengdu, sent him out immediately to start buying provisions, met the rest of the foreign team at the airport the next day, divvied up the tasks, changed the money, booked the transport up and down the line, found the staff, revised the budget, arranged for food and supplies to be purchased, remembered the visa extensions and insurance, solved a major snafu regarding lost glue, contacted everyone who needed contacting, solved another major snafu regarding a too-small bus, wrote my good-bye notes, got us on the road only twenty minutes past the scheduled moment, and reached Kangding within ten minutes of the projected arrival time.

It was an unbelievably smooth ride to Kangding: traffic light, the highway in reasonable condition, no breakdowns. All the folks I needed to find in Kangding were waiting for us at the hotel. My brick of money has only a minor dent in it so far. We have Yangjin and three new apprentices—college students from Kangding (Trajia will join us at Pewar). The foreign team has a very positive vibe. In fact, they make me feel left out with all their inside jokes, acquired during three days of shopping together in Chengdu.

Donatella Zari is returning for an unbelievable third tour of duty, an answer to my most fervent prayers. But there was an earthquake in Italy last year, and her husband Carlo has got too many other paintings to save. His replacement is Paola Azzaretti, a conservator about my age, tall, dark—a classic Roman beauty. Guido Botticelli told me ahead of time that he could come for only part of the mission—would that be okay? I remembered how important his contribution was last time, and said yes.

That's the Italian contingent. I have three others, volunteers all. One is Karen Yager, an American conservator whom I've invited to record and document the work. She's 53, Jewish, and very liberal. When I queried her on the delicate question of politics (I can't accept anyone who intends to use the conservation project as a screen for political activism, otherwise the Chinese government might cancel the whole program), I learned that she was one of those who, once upon a time, thought communism was a really great idea. After that, I asked no more questions.

Jonathan Bell is a master's student in Asian art history from the University of Paris at Sorbonne. He will write his thesis about Pewar's murals, which is all very nice, but I had a compelling ulterior motive for inviting him: he speaks both Chinese and Italian.

Last but not least is Kel Dennis, a 24-year-old Australian architect with a passionate interest in Tibetan buildings. Of course, I had wanted to invite John Sanday again, but he would have sorely strained my budget because he felt that he needed to work with a seismic engineer from Macedonia, and both command a professional's salary. Even then, I thought I would somehow find a way, but then the Sichuan Foreign Affairs Bureau inexplicably decreed that they would limit the size of my team to seven. That forced my hand. Anyway, Kel seems a fine person, very able, although certainly not a trained conservator. I want him to document the alterations made to Pewar by Shongshong during the last two years. I can't give up the idea of using John Sanday, although the work is progressing further and further, and Shongshong is managing just fine on his own.

Of the local staff, I've got the veteran Yangjin, now a senior apprentice, and Mr. Wu and Denba from last year. The cameraman, Chimei Dorje, is new to us, but a veteran traveler. Our host organization in Chengdu has sent the lively and energetic Peng Jing to help out. It's her first trip to Tibetan lands, in fact the first time she has ever seen snow at all, and she's taking to it like a duck to water, adoring everything. The prefectural foreign affairs bureau sent a representative, Mr. Liu, to smooth any official wrinkles that may arise—he is a Chinese born in Tawu and comfortable among Tibetans. Both of them have a smattering of English—for once it looks like language won't pose a problem.

It's dry and dusty here, not too cold but still winter somehow. Today's warmth must have taken the land by surprise because it hasn't woken up. The rhythm of the road induces me to let go of all my worries. Now that Kangding is behind us, there are few major problems that can spring up.

April 8

We've gotten over our last and biggest hurdle, Tro La at 4916 meters, and are rumbling down to Derge. For the last few hours, Yangjin has been sitting in front of the bus, on top of the engine cover, and I notice that she is starting to slump. How can she sleep sitting up? I wonder.

Something seems funny about her. "Are you all right?" I ask her in Chinese. No reply. I ask her again, and instead of answering she turns to look at me with desperate, pleading eyes, releases the bar she has been hanging onto, and collapses.

"Stop!" I shout to the driver, reaching out to catch her before she hits the floor. The bus screeches to a halt while everyone jumps up in alarm. Denba and Peng Jing are closest; they take her from me and lay her out on one of the seats. Yangjin's face is pale, eyes half closed, and she can't seem to speak.

"What's going on? What's wrong?" I ask frantically. Denba and Peng Jing are holding her so she doesn't slip down to the floor. "She has a weak heart," Denba tells me; "She can't stand the elevation." This is amazing news, for no one ever told me anything was wrong with Yangjin's heart. She has been over this pass with me four times, and never had a problem. "What can we do? What do you need?" people are saying to the poor, barely conscious girl. After a moment Yangjin opens her mouth and murmurs, "I'm cold. . . ."

Instantly, everyone is shucking jackets and piling them on her. Mr. Wu produces a jar of tea, which they put to her lips. She takes a little sip, but can swallow no more. "I just want to rest, let me rest," she begs weakly, closing her eyes. This throws Paola, one of the conservators, into a frenzy, for she apparently believes that if Yangjin sleeps at this altitude she will never wake up. "Don't let her sleep! Don't let her sleep!" Paola shouts in English, which few people understand but which adds to the overall agitation.

I try to get Paola calmed down, while worrying feverishly what to do next. I know nothing of cardiology, but it seems to me that a heart gone into overdrive (tachycardia) would explain what's happening to Yangjin. We have nothing in our medical kit for such an emergency. Derge and its hospital are still several hours away. Denba, smart and clear headed as usual, is thinking along the same lines. "We should go as fast as possible to Derge," he says. We tell the driver to get going. The bus resumes its downward rumble. People are crowded around Yangjin, chafing her hands, holding her with a reassuring grip.

Half an hour later the patient is looking better. She is able to speak a little and swallows some tea. An hour later, she's sitting up unassisted. Two hours later, Yangjin is perky enough to come out with a weak joke. I'm so relieved: it looks like she's not going to die after all. By the time we reach Derge, she's back to normal and will stay that way throughout the trip.

April 10

I reached Pewar Monastery today, in a chase car that followed the main party, arriving one day later, as I was detained in Derge by meetings. The monastery is abuzz, my team spread out all over the building preparing to start work. In one room, a student hangs wires for lights. The little Yamaha generator that I brought here in 1995 is still going strong. (We donated a twin of it to Palpung). Every mission has brought out more wire, lights, and fixtures. All our sleeping and eating rooms have lights, as well as our work spaces and Tenzeng Nyima's house up the hill, with enough wire left over to pull temporary lights to the back corners of the main temple. The wires are unsightly but no one would trade our electricity for anything, so vital is it to morale and work.

Next door, carpenters are building beds for us; in another room architect Kel and two of the new students are organizing the larder. Some carpenters are hammering together a work-table for the conservators to use. I relish the feeling of boundless possibility that comes from having so many skilled people on call.

Outside, a surprise: a new temple going up. Timber is piled high, wood chips flood the earth, and a mill screeches all day long. This building project, I learn, is funded by Pewar Rinpoche's newfound international supporters, for last year he was issued a passport and took up globe-trotting. Like many exiled tulkus who minister to wealthy followers around the world, Pewar Rinpoche has found that being incarnate pays better abroad than at home. Although he rarely visits Derge or Pewar now, he does send money to benefit his monastery.

In our common room (this year on the west side of the courtyard), Karen Yager, Mr. Liu, and Chimei Dorje work on two Minoltas and a Sony that didn't survive the journey. "The manual says: 'avoid vibration

1998 conservation team, on the roof of Pewar Monastery. Front row, left to right: Jonathan Bell, Kelvin Dennis, Chimei Dorje, Pamela Logan. Second row: Tsering Penlo (student), carpenter, Karen Yager, Qimei Dorje (student), Peng Jing, Guido Botticelli, Shongshong, Liu Yibin, Deshi Yangjin, Donatella Zari. Back row: Lama Kunchab, carpenter, Paola Azzaretti, Shira Gyaltsen (student), Wu Bangfu, Guo Tao, Palden (painter), Tenzeng Nyima, Denba Dargye.

and dust,'" Karen notes astutely if belatedly. The fully recovered Yangjin stews some herbal medicine for conservator Paola, whose sciatica is flaring up. Denba sits nearby playing at dice. Next door, in a small kitchen, local Tibetan workers are making a new stove out of concrete and stone. The other conservators are elsewhere at the moment, awaiting completion of their sanding space. Yesterday they tried sanding on the roof, but found the air up there too dry. Kids run around. The faces of older villagers are oh so familiar. I feel like I've come home.

The neighborhood is much changed, and for the worse. Construction of our long-awaited road has devastated the riverbanks, which are littered with the corpses of trees. Trucks groan up and down, carrying timber to market. Now it's clear why the government wanted to put in a road. It wasn't for the monasteries.

A while ago, I entered a room to find warmhearted Karen Yager thanking Tenzeng Nyima for finding her camera by bussing him on the cheek. Pewar's bulky, bashful abbot was flushing scarlet. I told her sternly: "Karen, don't kiss monks!"

"But we were all hugging when we arrived."

"The monks were not hugging women," I countered. Even though I wasn't there, I am pretty sure of my ground: Chinese don't hug, Tibetans don't hug, and they *especially* don't hug those of the opposite sex. That goes trebly for celibate monks.

"But we all hug and kiss the monks in New York."

"This is *not* New York!" End of argument. But not end of problem.

Kel, the architect, is like a kid in a candy shop, sketching everything in sight. Jonathan, the art scholar, works with the conservators, translating Italian into Chinese. Shongshong showed up only this afternoon, having come down from Palpung. He didn't receive my two telegrams, didn't know we were coming. There is not enough gasoline for the generator, nor chili paste for Sichuan palates. There is no cook; last year's cook has gone to mind his herds. Shongshong proposes we hire a Chinese. "Wages will be higher but the food will be better," he counsels. No arguments from me: food is important.

April 11

Karen, Peng Jing, and I are awakened at 7:15 A.M. by the old monk Tsetra. Knocking is unknown here: he simply drags open the heavy wooden door and comes in, carrying fresh coals for our brazier. The rest of the team is lodged in twos and threes in chambers all over the monastery. Slowly, they drift into the common room to choose from a do-it-yourself menu of tsampa, bread, instant noodles, instant oatmeal, *droju* (Tibetan dough fritters), and dried fruit. Tsetra has churned up a pitcher of butter-tea that sits warming on the fire. Alas, our honey and jam went missing on the road somewhere, so we shall have to do without.

My first task is to meet with Denba to set wages for our five art conservation apprentices. One came from Chengdu, three are from the Tibetan School of Sichuan, and the last is a local chap. Their leader, Yangjin, is the most senior; others are newer, and with varying backgrounds and expectations, so the question of fair compensation is a bit tricky, but Denba deftly sorts it all out.

Next I go to the temple to find Shongshong, abbot Tenzeng Nyima, government representative Mr. Liu, and translator Mr. Wu deep in discussion. Art scholar Jonathan Bell listens in, straining to catch the unfamiliar Sichuan dialect. The problem is, Jonathan wants to photograph the murals. I have a nauseating sensation of déjà vu. I attempted to head off this difficulty by asking permission in Derge, but no one knew who I was supposed to ask and my best contacts were out of town, so I had to let it go. Everyone agrees that the abbot's permission is most important. After that, Mr. Wu speculates that the Derge Religious Affairs Bureau is supposed to make a request to the Ganzi Foreign Affairs Bureau. Liu belongs to Foreign Affairs, but he says he doesn't have the authority. Shongshong opines that we should consult the Derge Administrative Bureau, then reverses himself and says better not. Liu advises me to get permission first, then take the photos later. I suggest that Jonathan get started immediately, and Liu can hold the film until permission comes through. Denba whispers to me in Chinese that we keep some film back (and don't tell anyone, not even Mr. Wu), while Jonathan whispers in my other ear in English that we substitute unexposed film and keep the real stuff hidden.

After going around and around, we decide that I should compose a written proposal, which I do, scrupulously and at great length, in English. Liu and Wu then attack the job of translation. I give four reasons why photography is necessary. My canny lieutenants delete the one about documenting the murals for scholarship purposes, Wu deftly intuiting the government position on such matters: "If we want to photograph the murals for research, then we should pay." We three slave like dogs over this document, but in the end decide not to send it to Derge today, but rather to wait until one particularly friendly official returns to town. Tenzeng Nyima orders workers to take down the cloth that covers the murals, anticipating that permission will be granted in the end.

Just before lunch, an adorable baby girl arrives needing oral rehy-dration salts, which I fetch out of the expedition medical kit. Peng Jing, Donatella, Yangjin, and I take turns holding the baby while the family stands by, watching silently. Mindful of the scene's PR potential, I ask

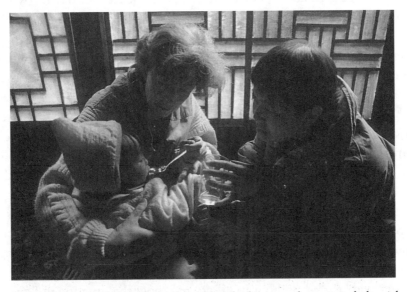

Donatella Zari and Peng Jing administer rehydration solution to a baby girl.

cameraman Chimei Dorje to film me with baby in my arms—but on sec-ond thought I wonder if this isn't perhaps a bit too much, as if I was running for public office or something. An old blind woman comes to ask for medicine for her eyes, but we have nothing to give her.

We eat lunch, the whole team crowded in the lively common room. Shongshong hired a stonemason named Huang to be our cook. Directed by Denba, who manages our food stores, Huang has made green root mixed with mushrooms, sautéed potatoes, turnips with fat pork, and a huge pot of rice. This is haute cuisine for these parts, and we scarf it down.

The conservators need the big room cleared so they can work. I relay this request to Shongshong, who dispatches local laborers to carry out sacks of grain, cement, ritual implements, and other dusty objects. The building is still undergoing reconstruction; it's full of the sounds of hammering and sawing. Workers haul stones and clay up the steep staircase. Peng Jing, Karen, and a student work for a couple of hours cutting sheets of gauze that will be applied to the back of murals.

Shongshong announces that he wants to call a couple of carpenters out from Derge. The carpenters we've got will leave in a day or two to plow their fields, he says. Donatella says that after the scaffolding is built, we don't need any more carpenters. I worry that we might need them after all, but nevertheless two sounds like too many. I tell Shongshong not to call them, figuring that if we suddenly need them we will find then locally.

Tenzeng Nyima departs for Derge with a shopping list, letters to deliver, and assorted other errands. Minutes after he is gone, the conservators report that the electric sander is broken and we need to buy another one, preferably two. One of the students is enlisted to make the run to town, which he will do by hitching a ride on a logging truck.

Lunch is barely cleared from the table when we are visited by three Tibetans from the township offices below Palpung. In these rustic regions where most men wear traditional garb, the ringleader, Ren Dekang, stands out in leather-jacketed splendor. He is coauthor of a book about Derge, and he takes an hour to talk to me about the situation in Babang township.

CHAPTER 15

DENBA TSERING, the greatest of the Derge kings, is memorialized in the southeastern corner of Pewar's lantern. In the painting, his gilt-roofed palace occupies the lowest floor of a giant palace—it's small but, tellingly, it holds up the entire structure. This one square foot of mural is a window to the past, to Denba Tsering's lavish court.

The king is corpulent, dressed in layers of rich brocade in the monastic colors of yellow, blue, and burgundy. Sitting cross-legged on a throne, he is surrounded by advisors. Before him, arrayed on a table ready for use, are sacred implements, showing how he is remembered for the construction or refurbishment of many monasteries, and founding of the sacred Parkhang, or Printing House. He is sheltered on the left by a *chattna* (parasol) over his head which symbolizes exalted rank, and on the right by an *adhvaja* (victory sign) symbolizing victory of the dharma over ignorance.

April 10

"After Liberation the government gave a lot of support to Babang Township, but because of its geographical situation, it's still very poor," says Mr. Ren, reciting the Party line. While it's true that the Chinese have poured manpower and subsidies into Tibetan areas, many of the policies they implemented were disastrous—especially during the 1950s and 60s, when forced collectivization resulted in famine. But Mr. Ren, like most everybody around here, seems to have selective amnesia on this point.

He continues: "The people here are mostly Buddhist. There is one

151

primary school; we don't have enough students or money to start a middle school here. Teachers wouldn't want to come here, anyway; conditions are too difficult. The government considers education to be very important, but they never have enough money to support the school well."

I can readily see how delivering an education to Derge's sparsely distributed population is a big, big challenge for the government. At least now schools teach Tibetan language—a major improvement. Sadly, those now in their forties and fifties—including my friends Malu and Nyima Tsering—are illiterate in their mother tongue.

"People think that if their sons go to school they won't be able to earn a living, but if they go to the monastery, the monastery will support them," says the official. "So there are more and more monks. People don't have enough education to see that this is a problem. In history, lamaseries contributed great things to society, but now they are becoming more and more numerous."

These assertions take me aback, but after reflection I decide that they have a germ of truth in them. Monasteries offer religious merit, status, an easy life, and the Tibetan equivalent of an iron rice bowl. It's ironic that renunciation of material values is a way out of poverty for many young people—and unfortunate, too, for if Tibet's brightest youth go into the monasteries, who will do the work of society?

"What plans does the government have for developing the economy here?" I ask.

"First, we must support the poorest areas," is his very socialist answer, it being politically correct from the Party standpoint to consider the demand side first. But I want to know about the supply side—how can Derge generate more wealth for its people?

"Along the Dri Chu, the government is starting several projects to plant quality foods," Mr. Ren replies. "They will plant grain and other crops suitable for the climate. Nowadays planting is done according to the family contract responsibility system. The government will provide quality seeds. At first, local people don't trust new crops, so it's difficult to convince them to plant them. The government will do some tests to demonstrate their quality."

He tells me that logging of old-growth forest in the prefecture will be scaled back until, by the year 2000, there will be no more cutting.[74] The timber industry has been by far the biggest money earner in Derge and surrounding counties. It employs thousands of people, both Chinese and Tibetan. After it stops, what then?

A team of Chinese and Tibetan loggers hunker down in their tent during a spring snowstorm, a few miles from Pewar Monastery.

"The people should have a variety of ways to support themselves," he says. "Mining is one solution, but considering the environmental cost, the government has already almost stopped mining. . . ."

Hmmm, I wonder; can this really be true? There were gold mines on the road coming out here, places where in previous years I saw a lot of

74 As it happened, horrendous floods in central China three months later compelled Beijing to enact a complete ban on logging in Ganzi Prefecture beginning Sept. 1, 1998. The government decided that tourism should be built up as a replacement. Early in 1999 they opened all eighteen counties of Ganzi to foreign travelers, with no need to obtain any special travel permit beyond a Chinese tourist visa.

activity, but this year looked deserted. The mining had left torn-up river-sides, unsightly piles of gravel, and pools of water tinted by mercury to an appalling shade of green. It was horrible, but at least it seemed to be slowing down.[75]

"We have contacted some companies in Sichuan about exporting *chongcao* (caterpillar fungus)," he said, referring to a product gathered on the grasslands that is considered to cure all kinds of ailments. "We have no *songrong* [Matsutake mushrooms]—the kind Japanese like to eat—but we have other kinds that can be sold regionally. This business, however, depends a lot on rainfall."

All this time, the official's two slouching friends have been smoking and sipping butter-tea endlessly refilled by the monk Tsetra. Now they are looking restless. We fix dates for an excursion to Palpung, then adjourn, and the men file out to their waiting car.

Walking around the monastery in search of Mr. Liu, I stumble onto the conservation team hard at work. Guido and Yangjin are applying cloth to the back of a mural. The new students watch closely. Others crowd around with cameras. Guido holds forth in Italian, which Yangjin under-stands using telepathy developed during the 1996 mission. Peng Jing translates Chinese comments for Karen. Snow is coming through the sky-light, so student Trajia is dispatched to cover it with plastic.

Shongshong mentions again his completely unaltered plan to sum-mon two carpenters from Derge. I sigh and acquiesce.

Batru, our cook from last time, returns from the high pastures and says he'd like to work for us again. At first I am happy to take him on, but then Shongshong says that we're already committed to Huang, the Chinese cook. After Batru leaves the room, Shongshong informs me that in 1996, after we were gone, Batru took all the leftover food, which he was most certainly not supposed to do. So we are not hiring Batru, an easy decision to make because Huang's cooking is superior.

75 Later, after the commercial logging ban of September 1998, the government would identify mining as one of the key industries to be developed in Ganzi. However it appears that gold is nearly mined out, so they will have to exploit other minerals. Other industries being promoted are traditional medicines, hydroelectricity, and tourism.

At five-thirty in the afternoon it's snowing, and even my three pairs of pants don't keep out the cold. The sounds of drumming, hammering, and voices are all around the monastery.

Socializing after dinner.

After dinner, we remain in the comforting warmth of the common room to play card games, give each other language lessons, nibble on snacks, and sip wine. "This is the most important space, after the temple," observes Kel, who sees every human habitation from a mystical architect's viewpoint, a flux of air, light, form, and human interaction. He has been sketching and photographing the monastery, new parts as well as old.

Tonight, with the help of Peng Jing and one of the students, Kel probes Shongshong about Tibetan architecture. The two builders take turns sketching in Kel's book, communicating in the language of structure and fabric, timber and stone. "What does this mean?" asks Kel, pointing to a feature in Shongshong's drawing of a column.

"Tashi Delek" replies the old engineer. The words are a common

Tibetan greeting, a wish of good fortune. Kel dutifully notes it down.

"What about this one?" he asks, pointing to something else.

"Tashi Delek" says Shongshong.

"And this?"

"Tashi Delek." Shongshong's face is transmogrifying into one of those embarrassed Tibetan smiles that I recognize. It means "I know what I'm

TYPICAL DESIGN OF COLUMN & CAPITAL

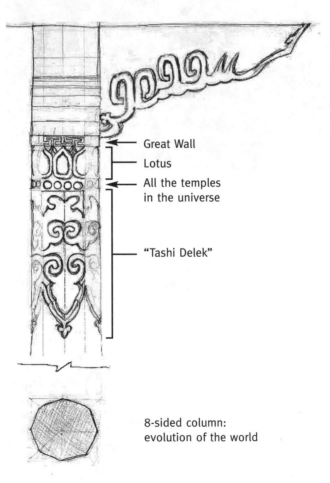

Great Wall

Lotus

All the temples in the universe

"Tashi Delek"

8-sided column: evolution of the world

saying sounds ridiculous, and you couldn't possibly understand, and I can't possibly explain, but it really is the answer."

Meanwhile, Chimei Dorje, Trajia, and Denba help me unravel the mysteries of the Derge dialect. The four conservators and Jonathan are absorbed in a far-flung discussion of philosophy and art. At eleven or so, Denba switches off the generator, signaling the day's end.

April 12

Today we saw the first mural released from its bandage of gauze. Guido was unstoppable, laboring right through lunch. *"Siamo qui per lavorare!"* he thundered (We're here to work!), spurring everyone on; even Denba was moved to rise from his couch and witness the event. Students fetch water, wield sponges, stoke the fire, and clean wood pulp, while the photographic contingent hovers in the periphery.

Paola praises the apprentices: "The students are really intelligent; they learn absolutely fast." Yangjin has a sure hand. Peng Jing isn't supposed to be a student but she's helping anyway; she's taken to this whole enterprise like a duck to water—amazing for a girl who's never left the lowlands. At last I've got a team in which everybody—absolutely everybody—is good.[76]

After the day's work is done, a bunch of us—Jonathan and Kel, Shongshong, Mr. Liu, Donatella, Denba, Karen, student Tsering Penlo, and I—somehow wind up in the lower temple with a pair of fluorescent tubes, connected by trailing wires to the generator outside. Using these magic wands of light, we examine the murals as perhaps no one has examined them since they were made. Under the scrutiny of nine pairs of eyes, nine sets of perceptions, nine times combined intelligence (and nearly as many cultures) a richness of detail suddenly springs out from the walls. No

---

76 I have no illusions that some of them—perhaps most of them—were under instructions to report the activities of the foreign team to the Chinese authorities. Certainly Mr. Liu, Denba, and our police escorts played that role. Fortunately, the role didn't conflict with our mission of saving Pewar's murals. In truth, I glad that the government was receiving first-hand reports about our wholly innocuous activities, because it enhanced their trust in my program.

Cleaning glue from a de-gauzed mural.
Left to right: Deshi Yangjin, Tseren Penlo (student), Paola Azzaretti,
Guido Botticelli.

matter how many times I look at these paintings, their wonder still increases.

Now I absorb the fastasmagoric multiplicity: a woman on a flying carpet, a doctor waiting between a woman's legs for a baby to pop out, a chain of carts held up by clouds, a warrior carrying a musket, Mongol helmets, Indian saris, Chinese tile roofs, large plump figures next to small hardy ones, a grand assembly of spangle-robed lamas, a Tibetan and Chinese facing each other in battle. In one panel, there's a pantheon of white-turbaned Indic sages. In the next, something completely different:

Asian figures, larger, with receding hairlines. The richness of the depictions, how numerous they are—it's way too much to get my mind around. But I take no small amount of joy from knowing that I helped save these paintings.

Jonathan Bell, the Asian art history student, has been in here every day, photographing and studying the murals. Villagers and monks can't quite figure out what he's up to. That scholars abroad are interested in their religious culture is a big mental leap for Tibetan peasants. Jonathan reports, "I've been interviewing the monks about the stories in the murals, and they don't seem to understand why. They were surprised. They said, 'You're really interested in this, aren't you?' Then later they said, 'You know quite a lot about this, don't you?'"

Later on, in response to my egging, Jonathan delivers a mini-lecture to the rest of us infidel foreigners. "The content of the murals is that of the Jâtaka tales," he explains, "that is, stories of the Buddha's many lives. The style is greatly influenced by thirteenth- and fourteenth-century mural painting in far eastern China. The paintings were done by a studio, which had a master who would outline the more important figures. Then his students would do different parts—one would do trees, one would do wildlife, jewelry, clothing, and so on. Then the master would return and put on finishing touches.

"Something really interesting: the upstairs murals, the ones we're restoring, it's as if another hand did parts of them, because you find some Bönpo[77] style that's completely different from Buddhist iconography. If you take a religion like Buddhism that comes from somewhere else, you try to make it as homey as possible, so Buddhism was blended with Bön. In the murals downstairs they were probably recounting a lot of Mongolian encounters. There is one Mongolian figure who probably represents the adoption of Buddhism by Mongolia.

"Development of each painting is from the bottom to the top, starting with the mundane—architecture, daily scenes of horses pulling plows—up to the more ethereal where you have all these Buddhas.

---

77 See Appendix III for more on Bön. Given the different styles and treatment of composition present in these upper murals—in contrast to those downstairs and in the Gonpo shrine room—it is also possible that these murals were painted later.

"Something that's very interesting, which is apparently a Tibetan characteristic, is that a lot of the stories have no order. They jump around. In the rest of China, the order of the stories may differ, but within one story the scenes are in some order, normally consecutive. They can be boustrophedonic. . . ."

Here I have to ask Jonathan to repeat that word, and spell it. He explains that it means the story starts at the bottom of the painting and goes to the top, wiggling back and forth like a snake. "Anyway, here the stories aren't boustrophedonic at all. One scene can be as much as 300 centimeters from another scene, and even divided by the scene of another story.

"In the main temple, there's only one esoteric figure, a gonpo figure, and it's covered. You know esoteric figures—lots of arms, skulls, fierce figures standing on people. That's what you call the esoteric form. It's used to help meditation. When you have all these hands and arms, or in *yabyum* with the *shakti*,[78] that's to help you to understand the nature of the deity. A lot of times they appear very monstrous, but really their nature is friendly. They attack ignorance, protect Buddhism.

"There are a lot of references to death in the murals. Death in Buddhism is a lot like the death card in Tarot. Death means change. When you see death in Buddhism it means that everything is impermanent: the wheel is turning.

"That little room upstairs is completely devoted to Gonpo, the protector of Buddhism. They have a small Gonpo statue; it's 700 years old. The other day two of the monks were showing it to me, and Tenzeng Nyima came in. He was shocked. They locked the door so no one else could come in. The statue was only about 40 centimeters high. Some gold, some blue, red. A lot of the colors were faded. Very fierce, tongue coming out, with sharp teeth—really nice.

"Tibetans adopted a lot of Hindu characteristics in representing gods; that's why you see a lot of demons standing on corpses. Gonpo is Kali, you know. Kali is really a feminist figure. You have Kuvera being stepped on, showing how Buddhism was victorious over Hinduism. Hinduism

78 *Shakti* means consort, and *yabyum* refers to sexual coupling that symbolizes "the process whereby the passive male aspect of ultimate reality is brought into manifestation by the powerfully creative female aspect." (John Snelling, *The Buddhist Handbook*, page 94.)

has the holy trinity of Shiva, Brahma, and Vishnu. In Buddhism you have the trinity of past, present, and future Buddha. Three is a special number all over the world."

A brief, contemplative pause.

"Buddhism is deep," he adds as a joke, and the lecture is over.

April 15, Palpung

We came out here somewhat unexpectedly. Guido has never been, and I promised to get him here before he goes back to Italy. But there was a blizzard on the day of our planned trip, and we figured Palpung, at a good 600 meters higher than Pewar, must be buried. Not an auspicious day for a journey. Besides, we had no transport suitable for such a grand and valued personage as Guido.

A few days later, with just two days left before Guido's departure, the snow melted and a truck appeared. Guido was game, so we took a bumpy, open-air ride under brilliant spring sun.

I have not been here for two years. Their repair money has run out, and despite the new wood, the place still wears a look of derelict grandeur, for major sections are still tilting earthward. We tour the building, finishing at the highest part, a balcony that overlooks the *cella* containing a gargantuan clay Maitreya. Above Maitreya's forehead, on a strip of wall, are nine round murals containing graceful blue figures in the airy Karma Gadris style. "They were painted by the Eighth Situ Rinpoche," Shongshong says to Guido via a chain of interpreters. "One night he had a dream, and when he woke he came here and started painting."

The Eighth Tai Situpa Chokyi Jungne (1700–1774), also called Situ Panchen, was an influential scholar-artist who made many innovations in the Karma Gadris school.[79] But could these paintings really date from the eighteenth century? When I came here with Donatella and Carlo in

79 Situ Panchen recorded in his biography that, when he went to King Denba Tsering with a request for permission and funds to construct Palpung, he presented to the king a set of thankas of the Eight Great Adepts, one of many noted works. (*Worlds of Transformation: Tibetan Art of Wisdom and Compassion*, Marylin M. Rhie and Robert A. F. Thurman, Tibet House, New York and the Shelley and Donald Rubin Foundation, 1999. p. 101.)

1995, the two conservators took a look at Shongshong's behest, and reported scathingly that the murals could not be more than fifty years old, and furthermore were not of particularly marvelous craftsmanship.

Now Shongshong is all worked up about these murals. He delivers a muddy prologue in his iambic Chinese before getting to the point: "Please, can you send some experts to Palpung to detach these paintings?"

I briefly consider questions of time, manpower, and materials, and arrive at a familiar conclusion: Pewar is more important. "No, I don't think so, Shongshong. I'm really sorry, but not this time. Maybe next year some of the students can do it. The monastery could hire Trajia or Yangjin—"

Shongshong shakes his head. "No, the murals can't wait until next year. It has to be done next *month*. If the experts can't do it, then can you please leave some materials behind? We'll do it ourselves."

While I'm mulling over the far-fetched notion of Shongshong detaching paintings, and puzzling over his haste, we all go down to pay a call on Urgyen Rinpoche. The boy has grown. He is starting to have a look of seriousness, but still breaks out into that angelic smile that I remember so well. He remembers me, too.

We say our good-byes to Guido, who will go back to Pewar tonight and leave for Chengdu the day after tomorrow. Peng Jing and Mr. Liu will accompany him, and I won't see them again until long after the mission is over. Meanwhile, Jonathan, Kel, and I will remain a few days here at Palpung.

I've never visited Palpung before in this early season, when the place revels in its lofty elevation, 3950 meters (12,959 feet) above sea level. The air is misty and snow blankets the encircling ring of peaks. Sunlight falls like molten steel. Weather is thorny and fickle; storms come and go. When the wind blows, temperature plummets. We huff and puff at every step.

Led by Shongshong and accompanied by Jonathan and Kel, I inspect the building. We climb to the monastery's summit to look at its collapsing roof and plunge deep into the basement catacombs. Shongshong has done an amazing job shoring things up, but there is mountains more to

Urgyen Rinpoche, dressed for a formal portrait.

be done. Everywhere are rough edges, unfinished corners, ladders where staircases should be, daubless wattle, walls that don't quite meet, hanging beam ends, bumpy mud floors, piles of wood shavings, tamarisk branches awaiting installation, open windows, and, in my old quarters, a door opening straight out to a ten-meter dead drop. Outside is a mess, too: piled logs, broken glass, scattered garbage.

We lodge in the former students' wing, for all the students have moved to the newly finished *shedra* (College of Buddhism) up the hill. Each morning, the monks bring us a basin of washing water. Lunch and dinner is noodle soup made with rehydrated yak meat. We quickly polish off the goodies we brought with us, which are much reduced by my sudden realization that we have nothing but our food to give to little Urgyen Rinpoche. Three days later we mount some horses that Shongshong has arranged for us and ride back home.

As late as 1998, parts of Palpung were still falling down. Here, Kel Dennis inspects the summit of the building, which contained murals later detached by the team.

April 18

The work at Pewar is plunging ahead. Kel, the architect, is filling up his notebook with sketches and notes. He pesters Shongshong with endless questions. Despite his fascination with Tibetan buildings, this is the first one Kel's really seen close up. Back in Derge, I took him to the newly rebuilt Gönchen Gonpa. As we entered the abundantly adorned main temple, Kel's mouth dropped open and he exclaimed, "They don't have anything like this in Dharamsala!"

"Of course they don't," I replied proudly. Dharamsala is not Tibet!

One of Kel's projects is to document the huge variety of lattices used in the sliding frames of Tibetan windows. A modest survey of Pewar, Palpung, and surrounding villages has produced dozens of distinct designs. The lattices, which are made with great care using a standard thickness of wood, look like snowflakes with their flowery symmetry and endless patterns.[80] One common type is an "endless knot" symbolizing the connectedness of all things. In another window, Kel sees in the X-shaped design a spread-eagle human form. Another window resembles a woven straw mat. And so on.

Shongshong tells Kel that every lattice is a mandala. A mandala is a Buddhist motif often depicted in thankas and murals. To the uninitiated, a mandala looks like a blueprint for some kind of surreal maze: it has nested circles and squares that are strewn with lotus flowers and other symbols. To those in the know, it is a symbolic map of the path to liberation. But the mandalas don't stop at the windows. Kel sees one in Pewar's floor plan—its nested rectangles of circumambulating path, outer building, courtyard, temple, and lantern. Each successive layer cleanses one of attachments as one travels to the center of the monastery.

Our team has been joined by a handsome young policeman named Dendawa. I figure that the authorities must trust me more than formerly, because they took their sweet time in sending him. Dendawa is smart, assiduous in his duties but good company nonetheless. His presence is an inconvenience to Jonathan, who has not yet finished taking his quasi-legal photos of the murals. Before long the whole team is conspiring on Jonathan's behalf: whenever Dendawa leaves the building, Jonathan rushes down to the temple to grab a few shots, while a lookout keeps watch for the policeman's return.

By now the conservators have removed facing from six of the ten sections. Guido is gone, but I still have three experts and five students. Might we be able to spare the resources to save Palpung's murals after all?

Donatella considers. She inventories the days left, our pots of glue and rolls of gauze, and who she needs to accomplish the remaining work at Pewar. Conclusion: Karen can go, and she can take Yangjin and Trajia.

I send a message to Palpung, offering to save their murals.

---

80 See page 210.

Pewar Monastery Main Temple (unconserved)

Site of a failed detachment test. The paint was not removed completely, and some color was left behind.

Right: Students clean mural fragments

Below: removing gauze from a large panel of mural

Conservators and apprentices stand on a scaffolding to clean murals in preparation for detachment.

Spot-cleaning a recently de-gauzed mural.

Pilgrims stop at a crude chorten during their circumambulation
of Palpung Gompa.

Expedition bus stops at Qiao'er Shan (pass) on the way to Dege.

Baiya Monastery brilliantly sunlit, against blackish gvlley and spankin' new.

Abbot of Palpung, Khepa Tsering.

Above left: Pewar Monastery Main Temple "before."
Above Right: Pewar Monastery Main Temple "after."

Murals painted by Situ Rinpoche at Palpung, before they were detached.

*Palpung mural in informal style,
featuring the Potala Palace.*

Pewar Monastery lantern "before."

Saraswati. South wall west of entrance.

20-meter high statue of Maitreya in the rear chamber of Palpung's main assembly hall.

Above left: Palpung window frame with timber partly replaced. Pigeons roosting in the woodwork took flight at the moment this photo was taken.

Above right: the author

CHAPTER 16

AMITAYUS, Buddha of Long Life, occupies the place of honor at the center of Palpung's nine round murals. He is broad of shoulder and vermilion of complexion. Sitting in full lotus, he is draped in airy blue banners and bedecked with the jewels of royalty. His hands in the meditation mudra hold a vase containing the elixir of immortality.

Longevity is thought to be auspicious, for it allows one more time to progress spiritually. One prayer to Amitayus reads thus:

> I prostrate to you who grant the attainment of life
> From a bowl filled to the brim with the nectar of deathlessness
> Which you hold in the center of your two hands
> Supple as the branches of a young sapling.

April 20 ✌️❦

Palpung leaders passing by on their way to Derge stop to pay me a call. Brusquely, they inform me that Situ Rinpoche's murals are destroyed, so we needn't bother coming to preserve them.

What? I can't believe it. I just saw those paintings a few days ago and they were fine. I ask the Palpung monks, "What happened?"

After a lot of overlapping conversation and arm-waving, there is a murky answer. The building is falling down, they say. The wall underneath the murals is collapsing. Workmen are rebuilding these parts. The

Palpung monks speak for a few minutes with Shongshong and Dendawa. Then they get in their car and drive away.

I am confused and dismayed. My heroic plan is annihilated. What happened? Could the wall have fallen down in just the few days that have passed since we were there? I ruminate during lunch, then afterwards call a meeting. With Mr. Wu's help, I extract the following from Dendawa and Shongshong. Contrary to my first impressions, the damage wasn't done by overzealous workmen, but occurred naturally. Khepa Tsering, I now learn, was waiting in the car outside during the discussion; he declined the pleasure of communicating with me personally. The only words his henchmen issued on the subject of possible repair were: (1) I shouldn't subject my people to the discomforts of the journey; (2) I shouldn't subject the work at Pewar to any interruption; and (3) the murals aren't that old anyway, so no matter!

That last point is quite a turnaround from the previously stated position of "please, please help Palpung!" What I am hearing now is: we refuse your assistance. It just doesn't add up.

With a great convulsion of brain and translator power, supported by my various advisors, I elucidate the following points: (1) Our people want to go to Palpung anyway, whether or not there are murals to save. (2) Although the murals aren't ancient, they will still be good training for the students. (3) They might be wrong about the murals being irreparably damaged. We might just be able to save them.

Trouble is, there are no longer any Palpung people around to hear these three points. More convulsions disclose that Khepa Tsering is due back from Derge the day after tomorrow. Via two different messengers (one of them is my old friend Malu, who happened to visit today), I dispatch the missive that His Abbotness should stop at Pewar on his way back so we can discuss possible intervention. Whew!

Regarding the Palpung monks' strange behavior, Mr. Wu offers the following analysis: Since 1994, many times I have promised them aid for the monastery, but I haven't delivered. So they're angry now, and that's why they disinvited us to save their murals.

Skillful diplomacy eventually gets the Palpung monks placated, and my conservators make detailed plans. Yangjin will lead the effort, with

Karen as advisor in case she runs into problems. Donatella counts the days they will need: "On the first day she has to clean the paintings. On the second day she has to fix them, put paraloid and vinavil on the wall. That night, before she goes to sleep, she has to put the glue in the water. Third day she does the first glue; one day later, second glue. On the last day, detach. It means five days."

Karen and Yangjin prepare the conservation materials, Yangjin eager at the prospect of greater responsibility. Denba at first wonders why I want to send him, but I soon convince him that he's needed to look after food and electricity, and act as Chinese-Tibetan translator. He goes through our stores, splitting what's left of our foodstuffs to feed the about-to-be separate teams.

We have a dance party that night, albeit without music. Jonathan dances a strutting fandango with Paola and a Caribbean hop with Karen —so zesty and sexual that I blush for the monks watching from the door-way. Then Donatella does the pair one better by taking a turn with the monk Tsetra, who is not pouring tea for once. Kel and I show a bit of martial arts (he practices aikido; I, karate). Denba's fast feet rap out a Kandze jig. Then Chimei Dorje, the video cameraman, takes the stage.

At 53 years young, grizzled and portly Chimei Dorje is the best dancer among us: his moves span the range from Tibetan folkdance to Beijing opera, from ballet to tango. Not only that, he's a natural ham, a party animal with an infectious laugh and a ribald sense of humor. Now, despite the small space, he soars, postures, and struts. We're laughing and applauding wildly by the time he is done.

Growing up in what is now Kandze County, Chimei Dorje's talent for dance was noticed, and he was sent to an academy in Chengdu at the age of 13. After graduation, he traveled with a theater troupe all over western Sichuan giving performances for farmers and herdsmen. This career lasted for thirteen years. It was back in the salad days of Communism when Mao's emissaries were Chinese Robin Hoods, taking land and goods from the wealthy and giving them to hungry, downtrodden peasants. Troupes like Chimei Dorje's were both entertainment and vehicles for spreading Communist dogma. How that message was received around here I certainly don't dare ask. Chimei Dorje is, I suppose, a Party member, although such matters never come up and indeed are completely irrelevant here at Pewar. His dance career long concluded, he lives in Kangding, has a position at the Ganzi Bureau of Culture, and does occasional freelance filming. He has a reportedly very beautiful wife at home, and two grown sons.

His dance finished, Chimei Dorje sinks down on couch next to me and pours a slug of *baijiu* into a shot glass. After some persuasion, I take a sip, and he clobbers the remainder. Our friendship thus ratified, he asks, "You know what my dream is?" He doesn't wait for an answer, but rushes onward: "I want to make a documentary film of my own. I want to make a film about the Red Guards who came to Tibetan areas during the Cultural Revolution."

I have heard about this plan before, from Karen, who despite the language barrier knows everything about all the Tibetans. Now I get it from the horse's mouth: "These Red Guards were Han [Chinese] people," he says, "a lot of them teenagers. After the Cultural Revolution was over, some of them stayed around. They adopted Tibetan customs, married Tibetans, learned the language, and never went home. They've completely blended in. The town Trango especially has a lot of them." His words remind me of a carpenter in the neighborhood of Pewar whom Shongshong says is a Chinese living as a Tibetan.

"I figure it would cost about one hundred thousand yuan to make the film. But of course, I don't have the conditions." By "conditions" he means money. It's a common euphemism.

Now he leans closer and informs me, quite unnecessarily: "I am a Buddhist."

I knew that. Virtually all Tibetans are. I've even seen Party members pull out amulets from under their sweaters, keep elaborate shrine rooms in their homes. Chimei Dorje goes on in tones of careful, slurred profundity. "Buddhism teaches that if you are greedy, if you have attachment to things—that's a pitfall." He continues in this vein for some minutes, using vocabulary that's way beyond my ken, but anyway I nod appreciatively. He smiles. "You and I come from different cultures," he says. "We have different customs and languages. But really we are all the same."

We are becoming more the same. Italian, Tibetan, Chinese, English—
they are all beginning to blend. In our small society here at Pewar, hot
water is universally understood in Tibetan, toilet breaks mentioned in
English, and meals announced in (what else?) Italian. Yangjin loves the
sound of Italian on her lips, trying it various ways: "Come si dice allora?
Come si dice Coca Cola? Come si dice Dona?" The inexhaustible Karen
gives nightly English lessons to our three Kangding students, and under
her loving tutelage they're learning fast. "How are you feeling? What
time do you breakfast?" they say to me, blushing sweetly.

April 26

The Palpung subteam, consisting of Karen, Denba, Yangjin, Trajia,
Mr. Wu, and Shongshong, goes off in a truck to Palpung. There is great
fanfare, many hugs. Paola waves a paint roller from the upstairs window in farewell as the truck pulls away.

I hope fervently that the work goes well and satisfies Palpung's can-
tankerous elders. Without a gesture of some kind there, I'm afraid we'll
never win enough trust to implement any innovations to protect the
building.

Work at Pewar continues. Jonathan, Kel, and I are conscripted in place
of the absent Yangjin, Trajia, and Mr. Wu. After so many missions standing on the sidelines, now I finally get my hands dirty. Not that I am
allowed to actually *touch* a mural. That honor is reserved for the real conservators: Dona, Paola, and the three boys from Kangding, who by now
are experienced assistants. No, we greenhorns are assigned *spugna* and
acqua calde duty, keeping the flow of clean, hot, just-enough-wet sponges
flowing to the experts and their helpers.

I blow on coals to heat the sponges, which sit in a cauldron of water
over a heavy firepot. On command from those at the table, Jonathan pulls
out a sponge every minute or so, squeezes out excess water, and passes it
over. "Not enough hot!" says Donatella to me in that imperious tone she
uses in the heat of battle, when human sensibilities are abandoned and her

whole being is focused on the painting. I blow harder, setting a flurry of ashes aloft to flutter over the work table. "I need heat, not ash!" cries Donatella, and I am crestfallen, chastened. Who could have thought that this job would be so tough? Now I blow carefully, scientifically, sending my narrow stream of air directly onto the blackest coals, changing angles often. Soon my nose is singed and I'm close to hyperventilating—

"*Brava*, Pamela!" The praise is sweet coming from someone who never minces words.

Throughout the long, exhausting morning, I blow on coals, ladle hot water, wring sponges and felt, tote fuel, empty and refill plastic sacks, carry away glue-soaked wood pulp, and translate repeatedly simple sentences like "I need [it] *really* hot." Jonathan is an old hand at all this by now, a teacher's pet it seems to me, joking with the two experts in fluent Italian. I'm Cinderella in reverse, demoted from exalted leader to ordinary *spugna* girl, and a novice at that.

That evening, we are visited by my old friend and mentor, Wong How Man, whom I have been expecting for some days. He is in the middle of one of his long driving trips across western China and arrives with his CERS field team, six men and one woman, mostly from Yunnan Province, all Chinese. They are dressed alike in blue and yellow jackets and matching caps that say, "CHINA EXPLORER—GORETEX." My people watch with curiosity as these manifestly alien beings swarm efficiently over their two Land Rovers parked in the courtyard. "They look like the bad guys in a James Bond movie," quips Jonathan.

I am glad to see my old friends, especially Wong How Man, but the staff is discomfited by these strangers. Policeman Dendawa gets into a lather about them, requests in his amiable but authoritative way to see their identification, reasoning that they *must* be foreigners. The real foreigners are pleased for the chance to speak English to someone new for a change. Wong and his crew bring beer and paté, eggplants and watermelon, film and reading material—all enormously welcome.

April 27

I go with Wong to Palpung in one of the Land Rovers. I'm eager to see how Karen, Yangjin, and the others are getting along with detaching Situ Rinpoche's murals. We find them relaxing in their living quarters after lunch. They are very glad to see me. My journal records, "The best thing that's happened to me all month was the scream of delight from my team when my arrival was announced."

And the murals? "Amazingly sensitive and fine pieces," Karen reports. "There's not a detail that's messy. But the wall's buckling. It could be a very short time before some of them are beyond saving, because they're losing large sections. They are mineral pigments, hardly bound at all. When we tried to clean them they lifted right off, like pastels. So cleaning was not appropriate."

Their household seems in good order. Denba and Mr. Wu are working well together, apparently having patched up an intermittent quarrel. Although the two aren't students, they've been helping out with the conservation. Denba boasts, "I've seen two years of this work and except for the chemicals, I'm an expert, too."

I return to Palpung three days later, this time bringing Paola and the three Kangding boys. They all want a chance to visit this incredible monastery, and the three boys would like to try their hand at an actual detachment. We travel by tractor this time: one student on the right fender, Huang the cook standing on the trailer hitch, Paola with her sciatica reclining regally on quilts, and the rest of us—including Shongshong and the policeman Dendawa—sitting on boards slung across the trailer-bed. We bump and roar for two hours, inhale engine exhaust, and pound our rear ends to jelly.

We find the Palpung dormitory dark and quiet. Our friends are out. We drink tea in silence, dazed after the blazing light and noise of the journey. Paola and the three boys keep putting their faces to the window, checking and rechecking the impossibly handsome vista that encircles Palpung like an IMAX screen. I know. I still can't believe it myself.

Our people soon return. They report that the work here has stormed ahead—only three murals remain to be detached. The Kangding boys will do it tomorrow. Trajia will instruct them. Yangjin shows herself to be a newly fledged master. Karen effuses, "I've been grabbing them, I've been hugging them; we've been having interaction like nobody's busi-

Karen Yager's hand directs Yangjin and three other students to adjust the position of a just-detached mural before scraping clay from the back.

Members of the Palpung subteam posing for a photo take time out for an imported American custom: the hug. Left to right: Karen Yager, Deshi Yangjin, Trajia, Denba Dargye, Wu Bangfu.

ness. It's been really powerful, really interesting. I went up to listen to the kids chant and it was like listening to the heartbeat of the universe."

"When she saw the little Rinpoche, she cried," says Mr. Wu. "She couldn't hold her tears back."

All are in brilliant spirits, especially since they're going home to Pewar tomorrow. It looks like it's all going to work out.

CHAPTER 17

On Pewar's west wall, south corner, the following story is related:

In the kingdom of Amara lived a wealthy Brahman called *Sumedha*. Disillusioned with worldly existence, Sumedha gave away his belongings, left the palace, and went into the forest. There he became a hermit, wore clothes of bark, and lived on wild fruit. As time passed, his hair grew matted and long While Sumedha was thus absorbed in the bliss of contemplation, at another place there emerged Dipankara, the Buddha of the past. It was announced that Dipankara would undertake a journey whose path lay close to Sumedha's hermitage. Arising from his trance and shouting words of joy, Sumedha sprang to join the multitude clearing a path through the country for Dipankara and his retinue of four hundred thousand saints.

As Dipankara approached, he was preceded by multicolor rays of light; the people's happiness knew no bounds. Flying devas spread celestial flowers across the sky, and the air pulsed with the music of golden instruments. As Dipankara approached, Sumedha spotted a place where mud would impede the Conquerer's progress. He lay down on the ground, spreading his long hair across the mire to shield Dipankara's feet.

Dipankara saw him laying thus, and halted the procession. Casting his mind into the far future, he announced a prophesy: "Behold ye now this monk austere, His matted locks, his penance fierce! Lo! He, unnumbered cycles hence, A Buddha in the world shall be. The mother that shall bring him forth shall be called Maya; his father shall be Suddhodana; His own name shall be Gautama."

And so, after many cycles of death and rebirth, Sumedha became the Tathagata, The Perfected One.

May 1

I sit on a dusty scaffolding admiring our murals, just unrolled and stapled to Pewar's east lantern wall. No longer a collection of gauze-wrapped pieces, they are a whole person again, standing strong. It's a great feeling.

Today is a day of successes. First, the boys detached the last three paintings at Palpung at a blitzkrieg pace. I arrived from an audience with Urgyen Rinpoche only just in time to see the last one peeled from the wall and everyone raise their hands in a victory salute. A short time later, Karen, Yangjin, and I mounted horses procured for us by grateful Palpung elders. We rode back to Pewar together, behind the truck carrying our teammates.

When we arrived at Pewar, I went upstairs to find everyone rolling up one wall's worth of restored mural, composed of several sections now glued to a long fiberglass sheet. A lot of people were issuing instructions to each other loudly in various languages. They carried the enormous roll into the temple, propped it up in one corner and started the ungainly task of unrolling it against the wall. Donatella looked around at me standing there with my camera, and shouted: "I don't need photos. I need more people!" So I ran to the courtyard, yelled at everyone I could see to come upstairs and help.

Monks, students, foreign experts of all stripes, painters, carpenters, and cooks—all were pressed into service. After thirty minutes of chaos the thing was unrolled and pressed against the wall by a line of variegated human beings. Seeing us all pinned there, Donatella and Paola made a joke of pretending to walk out.

Paola and a student got busy with staple guns fastening the mural to the wooden wall. At length we were able to step back and admire the thing. Shongshong and Tenzeng Nyima pointed to a place where two sides of a cut weren't lined up quite right. *You don't like our results? Call somebody else next time!* is what I wanted to tell them, but I instead I just shrugged my shoulders. At least no Buddha's face was sliced.

Some of the color is delaminating, creating little bubbles under the paint. Out come the syringes and vinavil, and soon we're all receiving lessons on how to inject glue beneath a bubble and press it gently

Students Shiro Jatsen, Tseren Penlo, and Trajia celebrate successful detachment of the last of Palpung's murals.

downward. Another question is what to do about the jagged white lines in the painting, showing where cracks had split the original wall. To in-paint or not to in-paint? It's a matter of taste, to be decided by Abbot Tenzeng Nyima, but anyway we have no time, so in-painting will have to be done later, or by someone else.

We have no time to fasten the north wall's murals, either; so Trajia is issued instructions on how to manage the task after we're gone.

When the excitement is over, Shongshong and Tenzeng Nyima buttonhole me in the corridor, wearing those awkward smiles that I know portend a request for cash. Shongshong begins to speak, but my impatient look has him short-circuiting some of the usual rambling preamble.

"With the money you provided, we have built many new rooms, and put in a new roof, and new columns," he says, translating for Tenzeng Nyima. This is nothing new to me. I've been following the construction at every step.

A pause while Tenzeng Nyima talks quietly for moment. Then, Shong-shong: "From the bottom of our hearts, we want to thank you for protecting the murals and saving the building."

More: "The monastery needs painted decorations to cover all this new wood. Otherwise it isn't done." He goes into excruciating detail about how many painters, how many days, and how many liters of paint at so much money per liter. Their smiles intensify as the speech gathers momentum.

Finally, the point. "Can we have 60,000 yuan for the paint job? That's not very much money."

Sigh. I tell them, as gently as I can, that Pewar Monastery is on its own now. The purpose of the program is to protect art, not to support the monastery. I can't be spending money on interior paint jobs while other monasteries are falling down, destroying centuries-old paintings. Pewar Rinpoche used to be an impoverished monk scholar, but ever since he got a passport and began globe-trotting, he's acquired a knack for fund-raising, as the new temple next door attests. He can and should take care of this monastery. My work is done.

That night I notice that Shongshong has moved out of the common room, and rebilleted himself in a room across the courtyard. Good idea; Denba and the other party animals have been staying up to all hours, preventing the poor man from getting his rest. Through the open door I see he has doffed his heavy chuba. The plain blue sweats he wears beneath make him look suddenly ten years younger. "Like your Uncle Joe," comments Jonathan, who has also noticed the transformation.

Now Shongshong stands on his couch, stocking-footed, making prostrations. It's a Buddhist practice, a familiar sight to me by now: palms pressed together pass over the crown of the head, then touch forehead, neck, and chest, symbolizing, respectively, desire to attain Buddha's body, speech, and mind. Then the person stoops down to the ground and stretches out at full length, reciting in alternation: "I go for refuge to my lama! I go for refuge to the Buddha! I go for refuge to the Dharma! I go for refuge to the Sangha!"

This physical form of meditation has a profound affect on the unconscious mind; it cuts through selfishness and delusion. As Mahayana Buddhists, Tibetans do it not for themselves, but to help all sentient beings.

When a Tibetan Buddhist wishes to express especial devotion, he or she makes prostrations along a chosen pilgrimage route, measuring every inch in outstretched body lengths. Some dedicated souls prostrate enormous distances, even from Kham to Lhasa, a journey of months or years. Once, in my travels, I met a group of such travelers. Looking in their eyes, even I (skeptical scientist that I am), saw radiance that animated and ennobled their every movement.

Now, at Pewar, I am moved to see Shongshong, with his hard-working old bones, making time for this arduous practice. He rises and falls, face earnest, sweat beading on his forehead. Tenzeng Nyima, that huge brute of a gentle soul, stands nearby, Shongshong's loyal friend.

May 2

Our last day at Pewar. I go through all our stores—food, equipment, chemicals—deciding what to take back to Kangding, what to give to the monastery, and what can go as presents to staff, monks, and villagers. Karen, who happens to be an occupational safety expert, helps me dispose of our unused solvents. The monastery is full of locals drawn by the aroma of a super-giveaway about to commence, and there is a nervous edge to the air. Painters eye lasciviously our Italian brushes. Paola and Yangjin get into a quarrel over whose favorite monk should get the last empty Tang jar. I pack up coffee and curry powder to go to Kangding, and assemble packages of food for needy families.

Meanwhile, everyone who is able-bodied and trainable is in the temple injecting glue beneath paint bubbles. For a while it seems as if the bubbles are forming faster than we can fix them, as if the whole wall of deities wants to fly away from the fiberglass; but by afternoon the situation is under control.

After dinner I pull out my brick of money, and with Shongshong's assistance start the complicated job of paying out all the wages. Delegations come one by one: carpenters, painters, cooks, water carriers, our delightful washerwoman. While this is going on, Karen is busy on the other side of the room, packing her bags.

Last on my list is Shongshong himself. I present the two months' salary due him, which he accepts, wrapping it up and stashing it inside his robe. Then he tells me forthrightly that he has received some additional payment from Palpung for his work over there. I assure him that it doesn't matter; I want to keep on supporting him regardless. I see tears leaking from his eyes, and suddenly they come to mine as well. He is so poor, so honest, so humble, uncomplaining, and devout. There is so much I'll never understand about this man, but what I do know I admire. The two of us sit there snuffling at each other until Shongshong mercifully excuses himself and goes off to bed.

And so my work at Pewar is done.

EPILOGUE: 1998

October 26

"Where did all these monks come from?" I ask Tenzeng Nyima. There are, literally, dozens of unfamiliar faces in the monastery. This is my eighth visit to Pewar, and I thought I knew everyone by now, but suddenly I am hard put to find even one familiar face. He replies: "Palpung, Dzongsar, Gönchen"—names of other institutions in Derge.

The draw is, obviously, Pewar Rinpoche's long-awaited and triumphant return to his traditional seat after a long absence. Despite his 65 years and frail constitution, he came from Chengdu at double-quick pace, today jolting up from Kandze in a tortuous twelve hours.

I waited for him in Derge town and joined him for the final leg up to Pewar. The route has changed greatly. The new road has been heavily trafficked by loggers, and they've been busy all summer. Coming up the Bei Chu, our headlights scanned pile after gruesome pile of logs—corpses of the vanquished wilderness. Yet my sadness fled as our jeep surged up that final familiar hill and squeezed through the courtyard gate.

Today is the sixth day of the ninth moon, the start of a Thugdrab Tagen empowerment, and Pewar Rinpoche has been anxiously expected. The village still has no telephone, so they couldn't know whether his arrival was nigh or whether a landslide might have stopped him days earlier. Joyful monks swarm about the jeep, jousting for the honor of portering his bags. The exhausted Rinpoche is rushed like an intensive care patient upstairs to a waiting chamber.

Baiya rinpoche leads preliminary ritual of empowerment ceremony.

The next morning, rather late, they get started on the ceremony. Tenzeng Nyima has been busy for weeks directing preparations. The obdurate abbot took out a bank loan to finance painting of the temple's new interior, and now it's grandly decorated. The monks brought out their silk banners and thankas and hung them. They created trays of *torma* (dough sculpture) and adorned them with psychedelic butter flowers. In the temple, they arranged cushions and low tables in long rows. They cleared out rooms and moved in dozens of beds for the visitors. They stocked firewood and charcoal; they repaired the monastery's giant stove and set up huge pots to cook barley porridge and butter-tea. They unpacked and prepared countless objects needed for the ceremony: red coxcomb headdresses, amphorae and chalices, butter lamps and offering bowls, silk parasols, ceremonial platforms, scarves of colored silk, and the sacred noisemakers: drums, bells, and cymbals. They gathered the juniper whose burning branches now send to the sky their purifying perfume. They gassed up the monastery's generator, and hung lights in the main temple.

Watching the hubbub, I realize: *We've given it back.*

Pewar Monastery belongs to the monks now. Vanished utterly are the transient foreign incongruities of women; cleanliness; Chinese, English and Italian; vegetables, wine and chocolate on the dinner table; badminton in the courtyard; nighttime dance parties. Now, the monastery is swarming with red robes. Tsampa, yak meat, *thukpa*, dumplings, *droju,* and butter-tea are the only menu. Thermoses are crusted with dirt. In a corner of my room—and I'm grateful that they saved it for me—I recognize litter from my last visit. What was once our storage room for conservation materials is now a monk dormitory. We saved the monastery. Now they are putting it to use.

In the main temple, Pewar Rinpoche presides over thirty-four chanting lamas. One of them is our former student, Trajia, wearing the burgundy robes and mustard-colored singlet of his primary vocation, suddenly all grown up. Most of the other Pewar monks are not there; they are backstage managing the nuts and bolts of the complicated ten-day ritual that has just begun.

On his high throne, Pewar Rinpoche seems not so much a god as an orchestra conductor. He knows just what to do and when to do it: chanting the mantras, forming the mudras,[81] pouring the water, flicking the grains. When he stands, young monks are there at his elbows to ease his old legs up from their cross-legged posture, and to spot him as he totters down the steep wooden steps. Leading a parade of grandly attired lamas, Pewar Rinpoche paces a solemn circle about a tiered platform loaded with sacred objects. He chants, circles, rings a bell, and nudges the young *traba* next to him who has missed a cue. When this exercise is complete, Pewar Rinpoche returns to his throne, collapses to his seat, then arranges his robes decorously. It's going to be a long, ceremonious day.

Above it all, in the temple's high lantern, painted figures stand watching. Seeing them now, unfurled in all their colorful glory, my heart sings and a tear comes to my eye.

I emerge from the temple to wander the neighborhood. Nearby, the new temple is taking shape, paid for with money Pewar Rinpoche raised

81 Symbolic hand gestures.

during recent travels abroad. On every footpath I encounter familiar faces: the old monk Tsetra who tirelessly poured our tea, carpenter Tashi Dendrup who in 1996 was also a conservation apprentice, Palden the painter, the woman who washed our clothes, scores of runny-nosed children. Kunchab, the skinny, inept monk who so exasperated Carlo and Donatella in 1995 is now filled out, majestic in the finery of a high lama. The villagers all seem to know who I am. They call me "Lo-bay," an unauthorized, Shongshong-coined abbreviation of my Chinese name. They say it and smile and open their upturned hands in a Tibetan gesture of greeting and respect.

This time my stay will be short. But I am a part of this place, and will be returning again to Pewar Monastery.

Where Are They Now?

The explorer **Wong How Man,** through the auspices of his China Exploration and Research Society, continues to roam the frontiers of the Middle Kingdom. Lately his emphasis has been wildlife; he has organized a project to document the migratory patterns of Tibetan antelope and other species in the Altun Nature Reserve, in Xinjiang. He lives in Hong Kong with his wife.

Shongshong is now working on a monastery on the other side of the Dri Chu, in Tibet Autonomous Region. He would like to repair more monasteries, if funds can be found.

Tenzeng Nyima continues as abbot of Pewar Monastery.

John Sanday, the architect, has been working on temples in the remote town of Lo Manthang, Mustang, Nepal. He writes, "I am pleased to say that the Mustang Project is developing into an expanded programme. Training of local craftsmen is our goal and we are succeeding! We are in the middle of the second season there." New projects on John's horizon are conservation of the Imperial Palace in Beijing, and a training program in Bhutan. **Razat Bahadur Pradhanang,** his assistant, changed careers from architecture to business and has married. They both live in Kathmandu.

Harry Wong, interpreter, cook, business management advisor, and equestrian, has been studying abroad, completing a program in the Waldorf education system. He and his wife **Lily** plan to open the first Waldorf kindergarten in China. They have two children.

The policeman **Malu** still lives in Derge. In 1998, he was named head of the county religious affairs bureau, a "promotion" that he regrets because the pay is less and the job more difficult. He is looking forward to 2003, when he will have accrued 30 years of government service and will retire to a house in the countryside.

Khepa Tsering, abbot of Palpung, may also be able to retire soon, as restoration of the monastery nears completion. August 1999 saw replacement of the last of the building's rotten timbers. After interior painting and fixtures are done, the building will be finished.

Carlo Giantomassi, Donatella Zari, Guido Botticelli, and **Paola Azzaretti** continue to pursue stellar careers in art conservation. Carlo and Donatella have lately been working with John Sanday in Mustang on the conservation of murals and statuary in Thubchen Gonpa.

Situ Rinpoche and **Pewar Rinpoche** travel constantly. Pewar Rinpoche returns to Derge at least once a year. Because of the flight of the young Karmapa to India, it appears unlikely that Situ Rinpoche will be issued a Chinese visa anytime soon.

Deshi Yangjin, chief conservation apprentice, moved to Chengdu where she is furthering her career as a painter. Her work was featured in a Beijing exhibition of young Tibetan artists in 1998. The next year she divorced her husband, and the following year became engaged to a Chinese artist.

Yangjin's father, **Nyima Tsering**, sold enough paintings to build himself a grand three-story house in an artists' colony an hour outside Chengdu. He still paints, travels, and exhibits his work; he also serves as advisor to the Sichuan government, and in this role continues to support preservation of Tibetan art.

Aga, who studied art conservation with us in 1995, has returned to his career as a painter and Tibetan doctor. Recently he enrolled in a two-year program at the Institute of Chinese Medicine in Chengdu.

A few years ago, the interpreter **Lhazom Dolma** reportedly won a long-sought exit visa, moved to Taiwan, and divorced her Tibetan husband. She shows no signs of returning.

Denba Dargye, deputy expedition leader, morale officer, and electrician, pursues some mysterious law-enforcement-related occupation in

Chengdu, where he lives with his wife and daughter.

Wu Bangfu, interpreter in 1996 and 1998, now works for the Kham Aid Foundation, directing its Kangding office. His wife Yang Li and daughter Wu Jie are frequent and enthusiastic helpers. He was one of the first customers for Kangding's new Internet service provider and is happy to receive e-mail at khamaid@ganzi.scsti.ac.cn.

Kunchok Dorje, video cameraman in 1996, has gone into business. With a partner, he opened both a shop selling Tibetan goods and a Tibetan-style teahouse called the Black Tent Café. He lives in Kangding with his wife and daughter.

Trajia, conservation apprentice in 1996 and 1998, has started a three-year meditation retreat with thirteen other Pewar monks. They live in the small chambers that Shongshong constructed on the roof of the monastery and will emerge in 2002.

Chimei Dorje, 1998 video cameraman and dancer, suffered a stroke one month after returning from the Pewar mission. His left arm and leg are partly paralyzed. Since then, he has been pushing himself to exercise, and thus making slow improvements. In 2000, an American physical therapist brought by Kham Aid Foundation gave him intensive treatments, accelerating his slow progress. He lives in Kangding with his family.

Buge, the policeman who was responsible for confiscating expedition film and video in 1996, is now head of the foreign affairs police in Derge. Since the region opened in 1999, his attitude has reformed completely. He now welcomes foreign visitors, and recently he helped Palpung, Pewar, and Dzongsar start up small guest houses. **Dendawa** works with him.

Zhong Yang, red-tape slayer, and **Peng Jing,** expedition paperwork handler, continue their jobs at the Sichuan International Cultural Exchange Center. Recently, Zhong Yang started a private company that imports technology for protecting the environment.

Karen Yager led a training program in 1999 in thanka conservation for Kham Aid Foundation.

Jonathan Bell, art history scholar, completed his master's degree at the University of Paris, Sorbonne. He is now enrolled in Columbia University's architectural conservation program and will work with Kham

Aid Foundation on conserving the murals of the Derge Printing House in 2002.

The author, **Pamela Logan,** has been expanding programs under the Kham Aid Foundation, which she founded, to include assistance for Tibetan education, reforestation, health care, and economic development. Up-to-date information about her work may be found on the World Wide Web at http://www.khamaid.org. She lives in southern California and often travels to China and Kham.

Acknowledgments

The Pewar/Palpung project owes its success to the hard work and generosity of many people. Top kudos go to Wong How Man for starting the program, something I never would have dared on my own. Volunteers for field work are relatively easy to find, but sponsors are rare, precious, and enormously important; therefore a huge debt of gratitude is owed to the following (in chronological order): The Getty Grant Program, Bureau of Mongolian and Tibetan Affairs of the Republic of China (Taiwan), Mr. Tom Yuen, Art Restoration for Cultural Heritage, an anonymous donor, Culture Charitable Foundation, and The Durfee Foundation.

The program owes its inception to three Tibetans within the Sichuan government: Luo Tongda, Tashi Tsering, and Tupten Nyima, all of whom helped Wong How Man get permission for and organize his initial field survey. Professor Li Shaoming also played an important role as program host. Later, Nyima Tsering was our behind-the-scenes advocate to provincial authorities.

The following companies donated supplies and equipment through the China Exploration and Research Society: IBM, Kodak, The North Face, Goretex, Fuji, Sony, and Magellan. Discounted and gratis air tickets were provided by Cathay Pacific Airlines and Dragonair. New China Hong Kong Group very kindly loaned a car and driver for some of the expeditions. Coca-Cola China provided Hong Kong office space, telephone, and fax.

Home office administration, although unglamorous, is crucial to running any field program. In Los Angeles, our angels were Craig Jones and Daisy Leung of Kham Aid Foundation, and Marion Fay, Mike Wong, Angela Holberton, and John Holberton of CERS. In Hong Kong, the weight was carried at various times by Carol Dille, Mimi Webster, Julie Gaw, and Berry Sin. Peter Klimenko and his staff at Kingain Industries helped out with straying packages and last minute problems. We would have gotten nowhere without the valiant support of Dou Weiping, Zhong Yang, and the others at the Sichuan International Cultural Exchange Center in Chengdu. Before Kham Aid Foundation received its status as a tax-exempt public charity, the American Himalayan Foundation graciously and expeditiously handled funds donated to the project.

I have already mentioned field team members in the main text, but extra applause and thanks are due to conservators Donatella Zari, Carlo Giantomassi, and Guido Botticelli for their courage and tenacity in traveling with me more than once to such a remote and primitive place. Other foreign field workers—John Sanday, Karen Yager, Jonathan Bell, Razat Bahadur Pradhanang, Paola Azzaretti, and Kelvin Dennis—also made significant contributions, as did our many Tibetan and Chinese coworkers mentioned in the text. I would be remiss if I failed to mention the architects who accompanied Wong How Man on the original survey: Patrick Troch and Yang Jiaming.

Publicity was enhanced immensely by Ian Alsop and Mark Hopkins at Asian Arts (now Panorama Point), who created a site on the World Wide Web for the project. Elizabeth Knight and Gene Chang brought attention to our work through their published articles.

This book has been much improved by the expertise of Kunchok Tenzin, Stephen Aldridge, Yang Jiaming, Josef Kolmas, Rebecca Edwards, and Nyima Lhamo. Wong How Man compiled invaluable information on Pewar and Palpung from Chinese sources. Translation of some other Chinese texts was done by Wu Bangfu and Jane Saw. Mark Lawrence read and aptly critiqued an early draft. The book incorporates many brilliant suggestions proposed by Andrew Stuart, my peerless agent. Last but not least, I am grateful to George Donahue for his support and care in bringing the book to press.

Appendices

∾❦ I: CONSERVATION TECHNIQUES
USED FOR THE WALL PAINTINGS
AT PEWAR MONASTERY

by Guido Botticelli, Carlo Giantomassi, and Donatella Zari

In 1996, we were invited to participate in the conservation and restoration of a very interesting cycle of wall paintings in the Buddhist monastery of Pewar. The monastery and the wall paintings were both in a very precarious state of conservation. The walls of the building, constructed using a mix composed of clay, had become brittle through the years, and there was much concern regarding the static stability of the monastery itself. Before work on the structural problems of the monastery could begin, it appeared obvious that we needed to detach the wall paintings from their original site. The detachment, or stacco, of the wall paintings would give us a chance to conserve and restore the paintings, as well as allow for repairs on the damaged walls. Our aim was therefore to detach the wall paintings, restore them, and replace them to their original site once the monastery had undergone its own restoration.

The Pewar wall paintings, considered one of the most prestigious cycles of Tibetan paintings, were executed during the eighteenth century. They represent descriptive scenes of Buddhist teachings and local customs. The execution of these paintings is considerably different from the traditional fresco techniques widely used in Europe and specifically in Italy. The main difference between these techniques is that frescoes are painted on a base of sand and lime mortar, whereas the Tibetan technique uses a painting base composed of clay mixed with vegetable fibers (straw). At Pewar, the clay had been applied in layers onto a reed matting, woven with small branches along a vertical structure created by wooden shafts (wattle and daub). The density of the first layers was quite thick, while the last ones were considerably finer and more compact. The clay mixture used for these last layers was composed of a paste which did not incorporate vegetable fibers. It had a density of about 2 millimeters and provided a soft, smooth painting surface. Prior to painting, the clay base was treated with a preparation of white clay (kaolin), bound together with a mix of animal glues or vegetal gums.

The wall paintings at Pewar, which we considered to be particularly refined and very well executed, were painted according to the tempera technique: pigments bound together by animal-based glues. Most of the colors used were mineral-based pigments, such as ochre, earth colors, cinnabar, minium, azurite, and malachite. We also discovered traces of red Lac, while we were unfortunately not able to identify the correct composition of the white pigments. Metal lamina and gold leaf enhanced the vividness of the colors used on these paintings.

The room at Pewar had three decorated walls, and our mission was to detach two of the wall paintings, a total surface of about 80 square meters. These two wall paintings were particularly damaged; not only had the structure of the wall, composed of brittle clay, started to crumble, but the paint surface had been darkened dramatically by layers of black-lamp smoke, due to the continual use of oil torches. In the past, these paintings had been treated with an organic fixative that in time had also darkened, rendering the painted surface almost illegible. These two walls also presented various deep structural lesions caused by seismic activity and by the building's static problems, and color loss was visible along these lesions. Damage to the roof had also allowed leaking water that washed the surface of the wall paintings.

Our intervention in these wall paintings was quite complex, not only due to the problems described above, but also because we had never before attempted the detachment of a wall painting composed of clay. Our main worry was that the clay would prove to be too brittle to withstand the mechanical stress involved in the detachment process from the wall. We were therefore forced to analyze with care the situation in order to create an appropriate methodology. We had to consider our resources, specifically the limited choice of materials at our disposal; we could only rely on the materials that we had brought from Italy. The monastery, at 3300 meters above sea level, was an isolated building far from population centers; we needed to use our imaginations, as well as our capacity for improvisation.

The stacco of a wall painting involves removing from the wall the film of color and its underlying layer of mortar—in the case of Pewar, clay. This operation is achieved by gluing a layer of fabric directly onto the painted surface, using an animal-based glue. For traditional frescoes, we normally use two layers of fabric; the first is a cotton fabric with a tight weave, while the second one is normally a fabric with a wider weave, such as raw hemp. Once the glue has dried, the entire surface of the wall painting is gently knocked with a wooden or rubber mallet; the vibration caused by this knocking leads to the detachment of the mortar and overlying paint layer from the wall. A wooden frame, previously built to fit the wall painting, is then used to hold, or rather embrace, the painting as it slowly detaches itself from its original site. In the case of the Pewar paintings, this wooden frame was not needed; the clay itself is a very elastic material, so we simply had to roll the paint and clay base off the wall.

To achieve a perfect result in the stacco process, a necessary requirement is that the painted surface be totally cleaned of dirt, fixatives, and repaints that could otherwise endanger the perfect adhesion of the glued fabrics. The delicacy of the technique used in the Pewar wall paintings led us to choose a cleaning method that consisted of applying a layer of Japanese tissue onto the wall, subsequently treated with a solution of water and ammonium (1000:1). The contact time of this poultice was a few minutes, enough to allow the dirt and fixative to dissolve itself. The surface of the tissue was then cleaned with natural sponges and cotton wool to absorb the layer of dirt through the weave of the tissue. The Japanese tissue provided a protective layer between the sponge and the color, allowing us to remove the dirt without having to directly wipe the painted surface.

The cleaning phase concluded, we began consolidating the painted surface to prepare it for the stacco process. After a few preliminary tests, we decided to do an in-depth consolidation of the color with a 3% solution of Paraloid, after which we applied a layer of polyvinyl acetate in a 7% dilution with water. The polyvinyl was used to increase the adhesive capacity of the fabric to the wall and thus guarantee the tension needed to undergo detachment of the wall painting.

At this point we were ready to begin detaching the wall paintings from their original site. First we glued (with an animal-based glue) a layer of calicot (cotton fabric) onto the painted surface. In normal conditions, twenty-four hours are required before the glue solidifies, allowing us to proceed with the actual detachment of the painting. In the case of Pewar, bizarre climatic conditions brought incessant rain that increased the humidity to alarming levels within the site and dangerously slackened the drying speed of the animal glue. However, after we spent a few days in worry and hesitation, the glue dried, and, relieved, we finally proceeded with the gentle knocking of the painted surface with wooden mallets. We thus began the stacco of the wall paintings—detaching from its original site the color surface, underlying clay base, and a few fragments of the clay/straw base.

The paintings were detached from the wall in seven segments, which were rolled into a cylinder from the bottom half of the painting towards the upper half. Then we took the cylinder into another room to prepare the paintings for adhesion onto a new base.

At this stage, the seven segments were treated from behind. In more ideal circumstances, the clay base, directly beneath the color layer, would be worked on until it became a homogenous strata. A second layer of fabric would be glued onto the clay base prior to the actual adhesion of the detached paintings onto a new base. However, when we began removing the excess residues of clay on the first segment of painting, we realized that we could not perfect this operation without electrical equipment that was unfortunately unavailable in the locality. Our problems with the drying speed of the glue had also delayed our working schedule, and we found ourselves considering whether it was best to postpone the last phases of restoration. We finally concluded that it would be wiser to return to Pewar with the required equipment at a later date. We therefore decided to store the paintings, still covered by the fabric and glues, until our return.

Our return to Pewar was not possible until 1998, two years after our first visit. To our satisfaction, we discovered that the paintings, which we had left in the monastery rolled along a wooden beam, were perfectly conserved. We were also delighted to see that the monastery had been entirely restructured, and wooden walls had been built where the clay ones had once existed, which meant that we could finally replace the wall paintings to their original site.

The painted segments were placed on a big roll with the colored surface facing down. Using an electric sander, we polished down the clay-base until it became a homogenous, smooth strata of about 3 to 4 millimeters, after which we dusted the clay and consolidated it with a 3% solution of Paraloid. A layer of calicot (cotton fabric) was then applied onto the clay base using a glue paste composed of polyvinyl acetate mixed with calcium carbonate. Initially, we intended to use an acrylic resin for this operation, but unfortunately it was lost during the horseback journey to the monastery; we believe it fell into one of the rivers that we crossed on the way to Pewar.

Once the clay base had been treated, the segments were turned around and the fabric that had been glued onto the painted surface was removed with the help of hot water poultices. The paintings, now freed from the protective fabric and cleaned from traces of glue, revealed all their recovered beauty and artistic integrity.

The paintings were attached onto their new base, a semi-rigid structure composed of polyester resin and glass fiber, and finally replaced to their original site. Our intervention on these magnificent wall paintings ended with the last two restoration phases, which included the stuccoing of missing plaster and pictorial retouching; both of these phases were carried out by the young Tibetan students who had participated in the conservation project.

With the collaboration of Prof. Luigi Soroldoni (Accademia Di Belle Arti, Como), Dr. Umberto Casellato (CNR-ICTIMA, Padova), and Prof. Achille Bonazzi (University of Parma), scientific analysis has been carried out on samples from the paintings at the Monastery of Pewar.

The procedures used included stratigraphic sections, optical microscopic analysis, and electronic microscopic analysis. Observations of the samples were made under UV lamps. The analysis performed with the spectrophotometer FT-IR has allowed us to identify the type of binders used, while the X-ray results have helped us to define the mineral composition of the samples.

These results have led us to believe that the painting base used at Pewar is composed of a mixture of clay materials (montmorillonitr-calcium and kaolinite) and vegetable fibers, applied in different layers and finished with a thin, white preparatory layer, also composed of clay, (kaolinite, talco and clorite) with traces of calcite. These layers of clay also include the presence of organic matter, probably animal glues.

The analysis has also allowed us to identify the pigments used, most of them well conserved and very much valued at the time; besides the usual vivid ochre yellows and ochre reds, we have identified other pigments, such as azurite and malachite, applied to the wall with a protein-based binder (animal glue), and cinnabar red and lead yellow (PbO), applied to the wall with an oil-based binder.

In the white layers, we identified a semitransparent strata composed of clay minerals (kaolinite) that, because of its translucent quality, allows the white of the preparatory layer to show through. A fragment of gold has revealed golden lamina overlying a thin layer of red bolus.

Further analyses are still taking place in order to complete the entire palette of pigments used in Pewar.

➷ II: THE GODS OF PEWAR: AN INTRODUCTION TO THE MURALS AT PEWAR MONASTERY

by Jonathan S. Bell

Sitting at the conjunction of two rivers in a remote area far from any population center, Pewar monastery might easily be expected to hold little more than a few monks and some religious paraphernalia of nominal value. Yet, there is a wealth of religious and artistic expression in the form of exquisitely executed murals adorning the interior of the main hall. The murals are unusual in modern Tibet in that they are virtually undamaged by time and humankind. They provide a superb and unmatched example of eastern Tibetan art of the early eighteenth century.

Access to this extraordinary body of artwork is achieved through the sole entrance to the main hall, or *lha-khang*, a southern portal of two heavy wooden doors that faces the monastery courtyard. Upon crossing the raised threshold and entering into the chilled darkness of the immense hall, one begins to notice large seated figures and pictorial narratives covering the shadow-enshrouded walls all around. Indeed, these murals adorn over 250 square meters of wall area at the ground level, creating an unbroken band 3.4 meters in height and 71.8 meters in length of placid Buddhas, richly bejeweled bodhisattvas and lavishly depicted stories.

Given the constraints of space, it is impossible here to examine and discuss this entire body of religious painting. Thus, this article will address only the general themes and composition of the works as they relate to their setting and the tradition of Buddhist mural painting. In addition, the discussion will be limited to the depictions at the ground level of the *lha-khang*, though paintings also adorn other rooms within the monastery, and the restored murals decorate the upper portions of the northern and eastern walls, some three stories above. They are all more or less contemporary and presumably executed by the same hand or group of artisans, though the upper register may have been executed later.[82]

The continuous band of murals can be broken up into separate panels consisting of large central figures surrounded by graphically narrated tales and devotional figures. The layout of these is completely symmetrical and is in keeping with other examples of mural work within Buddhist temples. (See figure on page 205.) The southern entrance to the hall and the northern portal that leads into a separate room with three large statues create a central axis along which the murals are divided. There is a total of twenty-six large painted central figures on this level of the main hall, thirteen on either side of this figurative axis.

On the southern wall, three large figures extend out towards the west and east walls on the respective sides of the entrance The figures closest to the door are guardians of Buddhist law, here seemingly protecting the sole port of access to this hallowed assembly hall. To the west is Panjara Mahakala or Gur-gyi mGon-po, patron saint of the Sakya sect and *dharmapâla* (*drag-shed* or *chos-skyong* in Tibetan), fierce protector of Buddhist doctrine. To the east of the entrance is Vaisravana, the king of the lokapâla, or temple guardians, who alone represents all four guardians related to the cardinal directions. Both masculine and warlike in their characteristics, they are contrasted with two stately female figures, Sarasvatî to the west and Green Târâ to the east, representing the attributes of wisdom and compassion, respectively.

Moving further out from the door along the south wall, we arrive at the final figures on the western and eastern ends and the first members of a group of eight that continue along the west and east walls. This group of highly detailed and heavily ornamented male figures represents the eight great bodhisattvas. On the western end of the south wall is Maitreya, the future Buddha. On the west wall are depicted Saranî-

---

82 The paintings conserved by Pamela Logan and her team are of an interesting makeup, some reflecting influence of Bön-style painting in the composition and two-dimensional character of figures. This treatment of subject is quite different from the murals on the first floor of the main hall. In addition, some of the works are recent paintings made to replace original artwork that was damaged or lost. Further research and study must be conducted on these particular murals and their content.

varanaviskambhin, Avalokitesvara, and Mañjusrî. Beginning at the south-eastern corner is Samantabhadra, followed by Âkasagarbha, Ksitigarbha, and Vajrapâni on the east wall. These bodhisattvas are beings capable of enlightenment who, so moved by compassion, have refused to attain their own *nirvâna* until all beings achieve their own enlightenment. For their unmitigated devotion to humanity, this group of eight is often the subject of special worship and devotional art. They are often found in murals and in thankas as central subjects surrounded by narrative and/or smaller devotional figures.

After the four bodhisattvas that adorn either side of the hall are seven buddhas, all seated and bearing the placid expressions of deep, ecstatic meditation. There is a progression from the fierce protectors, to interme-diary feminine deities, to enlightened beings finally arriving at the Buddhas themselves. Due to the symmetry of the two sides of the hall, the experi-ence of movement from the fierce and worldly to the placid and ethereal is preserved regardless of the circulation of the worshipper, though it is safe to assume that circumambulation would normally occur as elsewhere, in a clockwise direction.[83] The final two figures on either side of the north-ern portal are large Buddhas in gilded robes presiding over richly painted hosts of saints and other important figures. These four Buddhas, from west to east, are: Kâsyapa, the predecessor to the historical Buddha; Sâkyamuni, the historical Buddha; Dîpankara, the Buddha of the past; Maitreya, the Buddha of the future. With these four northerly figures, the Buddha, as an institution, is described, progressing from the immedi-ate past in the body of Kâsyapa, to the present and then presenting in more general terms the past and future holders of the post, suggesting an endless cycle of teachers and the renewal of Buddhist doctrine.

---

83 In a discussion with the abbot of Pewar, Tenzeng Nyima, on 15 April 1998, he said that the progression within the main hall (i.e., clockwise or counterclockwise) was of little consequence and that these murals could be read in either direction. Nonetheless, historically, these murals would most likely have been admired in the manner of circumambulation and some of the nar-rative depicted on the walls unfolds in such a way as to support the argument. In addition, it would be likely to have Gur-gyi mGon-po, patron defender of the Sakya, as the first central fig-ure encountered. There is also a small court scene under the image of Vaisravana said to be the court of Denba Tsering. If this is true, this would further support the notion of clockwise pro-gression within the murals, for Denba Tsering's likeness, representing his role as the commissioner of these works, would most likely appear at the end of the collection.

Symmetry also persists in the seamless background of these large central figures. The center four figures on the south wall are surrounded by other aspects or representations of themselves and by their esoteric companions. For example, Gur-gyi mGon-po[84] is surrounded by ferocious figures eating human hearts while he tramples cadavers, symbolism of the cemetery and the illusory and impermanent world that surrounds us. Each of these figures, mentioned in sacred text, has its prescribed position and treatment within a devotional image of Gur-gyi mGon-po. These figures are readily identifiable and found alongside representations of Gur-gyi mGon-po on thankas and elsewhere.[85] In this way, these first figures find themselves within their own prescribed environments, surrounded by usual companions and related beings, with some embellishments.

However, as one continues along the south wall towards either the east or west, this background changes. The final figures at either end of the wall begin to have their lower registers filled with detailed pictorial narrative, not necessarily relevant to the central figure. *Jâtaka*, stories of the Buddha's previous lives, and *avâdana*, parables and legends of Buddhist doctrine, are meticulously recounted here on the walls. This narrative continues around the east and west walls and to the end figures on the north wall. The four central figures on the north wall are host to grand court scenes of *arhats*, Buddhist saints, and others. Thus, these northern counterparts to the four figures at the entrance are also somewhat removed from the pictorial narrative that acts as a backdrop for the rest of the paintings. Rather, these four temporal Buddhas enjoy personal settings highlighting particular status or distinction. It should also be mentioned that they are painted in pure gold.

In addition to the narrative that continues around the walls is an upper register of small gilded Buddhas seated in meditation. This continuous band adorns the upper portions of the murals and extends from

---

84 Pronounced "gonpo" and spelled this way in the main text.

85 It bears mentioning here that a painting in an upper room dedicated to mGon-po, *mgon-khang*, is almost identical to this one and presents the same companions in similar positions. It is also possible to look in Tibetan art catalogs at thankas of Gur-gyi mGon-po in order to appreciate this representation and the strictness with which the order is followed.

the second figure on either side of the southern entrance to the third eastern- and westernmost figures of the north wall. It seems safe to assume that this motif is meant to suggest the one thousand- or ten thousand-Buddha motif found adorning the grottoes of Dunhuang.[86]

Let us now consider the stylistic and compositional elements of the murals as they relate to the tradition of devotional painting as well as to their public. As has been mentioned, the continuous mural work can be divided, for the purposes of study and interpretation, into panels bearing large central figures painted on a background of two different registers. The lower register involves the narrative that boasts its own earthly background of mountains, trees, caves, and man-made structures. The upper register consists of small Buddhas in meditation seemingly floating without any physical attachment to the lower register or the seated figure in the foreground. There are, then, three distinct planes of reality simultaneously depicted here within the murals.

This composition serves a number of purposes, both functional and pedagogical. The use of a foreground and background, differentiated primarily by size and the overlapping of the central figure onto the scenery of the narrative, establishes a sense of perspective and dimension that would otherwise be impossible in the relatively "flat" execution of this type of painting. It is immediately clear to even the untrained eye that the large figures dominate the entire painting and are positioned "between" the admirer and the other subjects of the painting.

Anne Chayet has shown that there exists also a general upward progression that results from the composition of this devotional style and also from the *horreur du vide*, or "fear of emptiness" that dominates.[87] The eye of the admirer falls immediately upon the central figure, then moves to the plethora of scenes below and around, continuing up finally to the ethereal field of Buddhas. There is no empty space within the composition, yet there is a clear division between the mundane, the register

---

86 A number of scholarly and beautifully illustrated works on the treasures of Dunhuang exist as separate volumes and as articles in journals. In order to see images of the murals, see *Tonko Bakkokatsu (Magao Grottoes of Dunhuang)*. Pt. 5, Tokyo: Heibonsha, 1982.

87 See Anne Chayet, "Remarques sur les représentations d'architectures dans la peinture tibétaine et chinoise," *Acta Orientalia Academiae Scientiarum Hung*, Tome 43 (2-3), 1989, pp. 205-216.

in which the various parables and legends are depicted, and the ethereal or heavenly character of the upper register of Buddhas. The central figure serves as a bridge between these two. Thus, the composition of the paintings has its own pedagogical value, demonstrating the contrast between the material world and the divine or spiritual.

The true significance lies in the main figure, already enlightened or on the path to enlightenment, but still clearly rooted in the world. In Buddhist thought, it is not the contrast that deserves emphasis, but rather the fact that contrast and even contradiction are one and the same. These large figures that, simply as a function of their size, play an important role within the composition of the murals are highlighted then for their ability to bridge two apparent contradictions. This concept, known as *panka-ja*, refers to the imagery of the lotus that stands so pristinely above the murk of the swamp and yet is deeply rooted within it, an obvious contrast that is not only easily overcome, but an integral part of the very essence of the lotus.

This triple plane depiction is also linked to the Buddhist concept of three realms, part of the overarching imagery and symbolism of the mandala. The Realm of Desire is said to encompass all humans and even deities still bound to the mundane because they have not yet conquered their desires. It is the largest realm and relates to the narrative that covers the wall. The Form Realm is home to the four immeasurables (impartiality, joy, compassion, love) and beings on a higher plane, such as the central Bodhisattvas and Buddhas. The Formless Realm is the uppermost of the three and the smallest. It is home to nothingness and beyond consciousness, concepts symbolized by the ethereal small Buddhas floating above the other realms. In this way, the murals also represent the mandala, divine picture of the Buddhist universe and the various planes of existence.[88]

While it is relatively easy to identify these pedagogical tools and interpret them, it is quite another question to name the style employed here. There is a style identified as Karma Gadris (Kar-ma sGar-bris, Tibetan)

---

[88] For more information regarding the mandala, see Martin Brauen, *The Mandala*, (Boston: Shambhala Publications, Inc., 1998). For further discussion of the Tibetan Buddhist concept of universe and other, see Robert A.F. Thurman, *Tibetan Buddhism* (New York: Harper Collins, 1995).

that originated in Kham, and according to some, was created by Namkha Tashi, an artist said to have been particularly influenced by the famous eighth Karmapa Mikyo Dorje (1507-1554), who was both an important reincarnation and an accomplished artist. This local style has been addressed most thoroughly by Pratapaditya Pal, though Giuseppe Tucci, the father of Tibetan art, had also identified a style particular to Kham.[89] Heather Stoddard has determined that this school was based in Derge itself and developed during the second half of the sixteenth century from the southwestern classical style Man-bris (sMan-bris), incorporating Chinese influences into the treatment of its subjects.[90]

Pal indicates that the Karma Gadris style is employed most frequently in representations of narrative, which dominate on the walls of Pewar. Figures are painted with Tibetan features and local attire, despite the fact that the subject might be Indian from the fifth century B.C.[91] This holds true for Pewar and, in addition, Indian warriors and other military figures are depicted in Mongolian armor, a recent memory at the time of painting because of the Mongolian rule that much of Tibet was subjected to just before the establishment of the Yuan dynasty. The murals reveal the application of a local interpretation of distant places, peoples, and events to make them more readily intelligible to the lay-person.

John Huntington notes certain qualities of the Karma Gadris style in his doctoral thesis, remarking especially on the high quality and originality of the style within Tibet.[92] He identifies an extremely expressive character that is complemented by almost painful detail that includes every accessory and line, even on the smallest figure. This particular treatment and love for detail is one of the stylistic aspects inherited from China alluded to by Heather Stoddard.

89 See Pratapaditya Pal, *Tibetan Painting: A Study of Tibetan Thankas Eleventh to Nineteenth Centuries* (Basel: Ravi Kumar, 1984); Giuseppe Tucci, *Tibetan Painted Scrolls*, 3 vols. (Rome: Libreria dello Stato, 1949), p. 555.

90 See Heather Karmay, *Early Sino-Tibetan Art* (Warminster, England: Aris & Phillips Ltd., 1975), p. 2.

91 See Pal, *Tibetan Painting*, 1984, p. 103.

92 See John C. Huntington, *The Styles and Stylistic Sources of Tibetan Painting*, thesis (University of California at Los Angeles, 1968), p. 164.

It seems a logical move to identify these murals as painted in the Karma Gadris style, as a broad identification. Of course, almost 200 years did pass from the time of its creation to the painting of these murals, and the style not only developed, but also must have fragmented into different schools and subdivisions. Unfortunately, until more research is conducted and there are more breakthroughs concerning the art of Kham and the rest of eastern Tibet, it will be nearly impossible to be more specific and name the substyle that is probably present at Pewar.

Nonetheless, the murals of Pewar offer an amazing insight into the artistic expression of eighteenth-century eastern Tibet. The most astounding characteristic of the style employed is its syncretic aspect. Not only is the subject matter truly international, but the treatment and composition of the paintings reveal influences from India, Nepal, and China. All of this has been realized with a hand that somehow remains distinctly Tibetan and, to be bold, expresses a dynamism that is unique to the centuries-old artistic center of Derge. These murals may be pivotal in the identification of an eighteenth-century style from Kham that is distinct from earlier styles. Further research must be conducted and the wealth of Pewar's murals needs to be recognized on an international level.

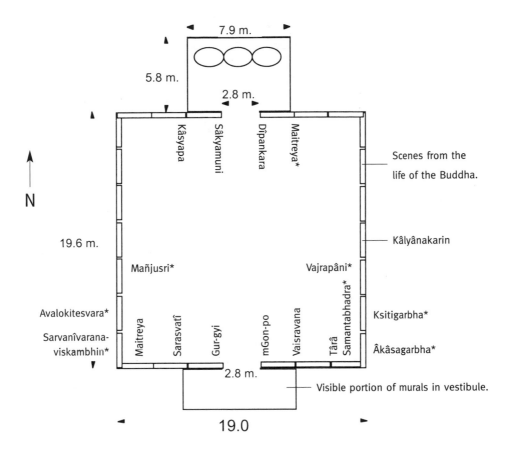

7.9 m.

5.8 m.

2.8 m.

Kâsyapa

Sâkyamuni

Dîpankara

Maitreya*

N

Scenes from the
life of the Buddha.

19.6 m.

Kâlyânakarin

Mañjusri*

Vajrapâni*

Avalokitesvara*

Ksitigarbha*

Sarvanîvarana-
viskambhin*

Âkâsagarbha*

Maitreya

Sarasvatî

Gur-gyi

mGon-po

Vaisravana

Târâ

Samantabhadra*

2.8 m.

Visible portion of murals in vestibule.

19.0

* The 8 great Bodhisattvas

The 3 statues of Dîpankara, Sâkyamuni and Maitreya

NB: The sections whose central figures are not identified are
adorned with large Buddhas.

INSCRIPTIONS IDENTIFYING NON-BUDDHA CENTRAL FIGURES

Southern Half of Main Temple
(Clockwise from Entrance)

1	གར་གྱི་མགོན་པོ།	Panjara Mahakala (gur-gyi mgon-po)
2	རྗེ་བཙུན་མ་གཡང་ཅན།	Sarasvatî
3	བྱམས་པ་ལ་ན་མོ།	Maitreya
4	སྒྲིབ་པ་རྣམ་སེལ་བ་ལ་ན་མོ།	Sarvanîvaranaviskam- bhin
5	སྤྱན་རས་གཟིགས་དབང་ཕྱུག་ལ་ན་མོ།	Avalokitesvara
6	བྱང་ཆུབ་སེམས་དཔའ་འཇམ་དཔལ་ལ་ན་མོ།	Mañjusrî
21	བྱང་ཆུབ་སེམས་དཔའ་ཕྱུག་ན་རྡོ་རྗེ།	Vajrapâni
22	བྱང་ཆུབ་སེམས་དཔའ་སའི་སྙིང་པོ།	Ksitigarbha
23	བྱང་ཆུབ་སེམས་དཔའ་ནམ་མཁའི་སྙིང་པོ།	Akasagarbha
24	བྱང་ཆུབ་སེམས་དཔའ་ཀུན་ཏུ་བཟང་པོ།	Samantabhadra
25	སེང་ལྡེང་ནགས་ཀྱི་སྒྲོལ་ལ་ན་མོ།	Green Târâ
26	རྣམས་ཐོས་སྲས།	Vaisravana

APPENDICES

Pigments and Coloring Agents Used

Color	Source	Formula	Description
Green	Terra verde (green verditer)		Hydrous ferrous silicate containing magnesium, aluminum, and potassium.
	Malachite	$Cu_2(OH)_2(CO_3)_2$	Alteration of copper carbonate occurring in nature.
Blue	Azurite (blue verditer)	$Cu_3(OH)_2(CO_3)_2$	Alteration of copper carbonate.
Red	Cinnabar (vermilion)	HgS	Mercuric sulfide.
Orange	Minium (red lead)	Pb_3O_4	Artificial lead oxide made through the oxidation of lead monoxide lacquer. The color ranges from light yellow to dark red.
Yellow	Ochre		
Gold	Gold	Au	Gold paint.
White	Kaolin	$Al_2Si_2O_5(OH)_4$	Hydrous aluminum silicate formed by the decomposition of feldspar and other aluminum silicates.
	Animal glue, milk, vegetable resins		
Black	Animal bones, carbon, cooled smoke		The carbon comes from vegetable pigments. The cooled smoke is from butter lamps, candles, and burned resinous woods.

III: A BRIEF INTRODUCTION
TO TIBETAN BUDDHISM

by Pamela Logan

Before Buddhism arrived, Tibetans worshipped according to the precepts of an animist faith known as Bön, which is concerned with mankind's relationship with a variety of gods, spirits, and demons. Bön still survives in Tibet, particularly on the eastern plateau, but has been so transformed by the influence of Buddhism that in outward appearance the two faiths seem almost indistinguishable.

Buddhism originated in India, founded by a real person named Siddartha Gautama—the "historical Buddha." After anguishing for many years over the suffering and injustice of the world, in the year 538 B.C., while meditating beneath a Bodhi tree, Gautama is said to have achieved spiritual awakening, or "enlightenment."

Over subsequent centuries, his teachings spread to neighboring countries, gradually expanding along trade routes to southeast Asia, China, and Japan. Buddhism's arrival in Tibet was comparatively late, and came in two waves. The first transmission began during the reign of Songtsen Gampo (A.D. 609-649). In a now-famous story, the Tibetan king took two Buddhists for wives, one from China and the other from Nepal, who converted their husband.

Bön priests did not take kindly to the incursion of this new faith. Langdarma, who reigned from A.D. 838 to 842, was sympathetic to them and initiated a period of persecution. His reign nearly succeeded in eliminating Buddhism from Tibet. Following his death and the 150-year "dark age"[93] that followed, a fresh influx of Buddhist teachings arrived

93 In contrast to central Tibet, Buddhism in Kham thrived from the time of Songtsen Gampo right through the "dark age," with several teachers from Kham contributing substantially to the revival. (Stephen Aldridge, personal communication).

from India, carried by Atisha and other masters into western Tibet. From there, a full-scale revival spread to central Tibet, and along with it, building of monasteries and induction of new monks.

The fundamentals of Buddhism lie in what are called the Four Noble Truths. Simply put, they are: (1) suffering exists in the world; (2) by desiring things (such as wealth, beauty, or knowledge), we cause our own suffering; (3) liberation from suffering is possible; and (4) liberation may be accomplished by adhering to the Noble Path of correct understanding, thought, speech, action, livelihood, effort, mindfulness, and concentration.[94] This much is common to all Buddhists. The rest is concerned with detailed examination of these tenets, especially practical methods for pursuing the Noble Path.

As Buddhism flourished in Tibet, it was fading away in India, so it fell to Tibetan scholars to preserve and develop Buddhist doctrines. By the fourteenth century, the complete canon—held to be the spoken words of the founder—had been set down in a set of 108 volumes called the Kangyur. Commentaries, comprising a further 225 volumes, were standardized as the Tengyur.

In time, differences in doctrine and practice arose among various Tibetan groups, leading to the emergence of distinct lineages. They are:

Nyingma School ("old ones"). This name was not coined by its members, but was awarded by default to adherents who remained loyal to the practices of the first transmission, eschewing later developments. Their teachings are codified in a 61-volume work said to be based on secret doctrines hidden by Padmasambhava in various locations around western Tibet. Before the Tibetan diaspora that began in 1950, the Nyingmapa had no designated supreme leader.

Sakya School. The order is named for its principal monastery, which lies in a town of the same name, west of Shigatse. It was founded in 1073 by Konchog Gyalpo. The Sakya sect became politically powerful in the thirteenth century thanks to patronage of Khubilai Khan. Authority over

---

94 These concepts are awkward to express in English, therefore this short summary is necessarily incomplete and perhaps even misleading. One very readable work that offers more detailed discussion is *The Buddhist Handbook: A Complete Guide to Buddhist Schools, Teaching, Practice, and History*, by John Snelling, Inner Traditions, 1991.

the order is vested in the title Sakya Trizin, which is passed from uncle to nephew, or (if the leader marries, which does happen) from father to son. The current holder lives in exile.

Kagyu School ("oral transmission"). The order originated with the Indian masters Naropa and Tilopa, whose teachings were brought to Tibet by Marpa the Translator in the eleventh century. It subsequently split into several subsects, of which the Karma Kagyu is the largest. They have a supreme head known as the Karmapa, whose traditional seat is Tsurphu Monastery. (Palpung is traditionally second in the hierarchy of monasteries, after Tsurphu.) The sixteenth Karmapa fled Tibet in 1959; he subsequently acquired an enormous international following and established Rumtek Monastery in Sikkim as a seat-in-exile. At the time of this writing, the identity of his reincarnated successor is still in dispute.

Gelug School ("virtuous"). Tsongkhapa (1357-1419) was the founder of this order. He felt that Buddhist practice of his day had become too lax, and urged a return to austerity and renunciation. Tsongkhapa's teachings won him a wide following that continued to grow after his death. In the sixteenth century, the Gelug school received protection of the Mongol leader Altan Khan, and with this advantage was able to displace the previously dominant Kagyu sect over most of Tibet. Now, the Gelug order commands Tibet's richest monasteries, especially in the Lhasa region.

Formally, the Dalai Lama is head only of the Gelug order, but the influence of that school, combined with the political astuteness of the fifth and thirteenth Dalai Lamas in particular, established the title holder as supreme leader of all Tibet. His religious authority is shared to a degree with the Panchen Lama, depending on their relative age and talent.

⤳ IV: TABLE OF TOPONYMS

Name used in this book	Tibetan name	Wylie Transliteration	Chinese name	Pinyin	Other names
Pewar Monastery	དཔེ་ཝར་དགོན་པ	dPe war dGon pa	白亚寺	Baiya Si	
Bathang	འབའ་ཐང	'Ba' thang	巴唐	Batang	
Chagtreng	ཕྱག་ཕྲེང	Phyag phreng	乡城	Xiangcheng	
Chamdo	ཆབ་མདོ	Chab mdo	唱都	Changdu	
Changra	ལྕང་ར	lCang ra	龚垭	Gongya	
Derge	སྡེ་དགེ	sDe dGe	德格	Dege	
Dri Chu	འབྲི་ཆུ	'Dri chu	金沙江	Jinsha Jiang	upper Yangtze River
Dzongsar Monastery	རྫོང་སར་དགོན་པ	rDzong sar dGon pa	仲萨寺	Zhongsa Si	
Dzongzhab			新都桥	Xinduqiao	
Ganzi (Prefecture)	དཀར་མཛེས	dKar mdzes	敢自州	Ganzi Zhou	
Göncheshi	མགོན་ལྕེ་གཤིས	mGon lce gshis	安吉黑	Anjihei	
Gyelthang	རྒྱལ་ཐང	rGyal thang	中甸	Zhongdian	
Jomda	འཇོ་མདའ	'Jo mda'	江达	Jiangda	
Kandze (County)	དཀར་མཛེས	dKar mdzes	甘孜县	Ganzi Xian	
Kangding	དར་རྩེ་མདོ	Dar rTse mdo	康定	Kangding	Tachienlu, Dajianlu, Dardo
Kham	ཁམས	Khams	康巴	Kangba	
Konjo	གོ་འཇོ	Go 'jo	贡觉	Gongjue	Gonjo
Korlondo	འཁོར་ལོ་མདོ	'Khor lo mdo	柯洛	Keluotong	
Lithang	ལི་ཐང	Li thang	里唐	Litang	
Manigango	མ་ནི་གད་མགོ	Ma ni gad mgo	马尼干戈	Manigange	Yulong

213

Mesho	མེན་གོང་	sMan shod	麦宿	Maisu	
Nyarong	ཉག་རོང་	Nyag rong	新龙	Xinlong	
Palpung Monastery	དཔལ་སྤུངས་ དགོན་པ་	dPal sPungs dGon pa	八邦寺	Babang Si	
Pelyul	དཔལ་ཡུལ་	dPal yul	白玉	Baiyu	
Serdar	གསེར་ཐལ་	gSer thal	色达	Seda	
Sershul	སེར་ཤུལ་	Ser shul	石渠	Shiqu	Dzachu-ka
Tawu	རྟའུ་	rTa'u	道孚	Daofu	Dawu
Trango	བྲག་འགོ་	Brag 'go	炉霍	Luhuo	
Xikang			西康	Xikang	Sikang

V: MONASTERY BUILDINGS AND THEIR FATE DURING THE YEARS OF TURMOIL

by Pamela Logan

The fate of monasteries in Tibet since 1949 has been a subject of concern to many in the West, but little specific information has been published. Palpung Monastery, for example, was reported by Chogyam Trungpa as destroyed, and, prior to Wong How Man's survey, even some officials in Chengdu told him that it has been lost—yet these reports turned out to be incorrect. The table that follows derives from research that is neither systematic nor comprehensive, but nevertheless may be useful to historians who are trying to sort out what happened in Kham between 1949 and 1980 when there were no foreign witnesses.

Some notes of explanation are in order. Whether a monastery was "destroyed" or not is often a cloudy question. Generally speaking, Red Guards (and those instigated by them) tended to go after the easiest targets first: statues and moveable objects, and these were lost virtually everywhere. The next step was to destroy smaller buildings such as residences and stupas, and eject the monks. Often, a monastery's larger temples—those with thick stone or rammed earth walls—were left standing, to be taken over by government or Party officials. Such buildings would require heavy equipment, major fire, or aerial bombing to destroy completely, and this occurred during the rebellion of the 1950s but was comparatively rare. In virtually all cases, surviving temples were not maintained properly: some subsequently fell down by themselves or had to be abandoned as unsafe. A construction boom commenced in the late 1980s and is now, at the turn of the century, winding down as the larger monasteries have repaired or replaced their most important buildings. In Ganzi Prefecture, which lists 475 active monasteries, it is now rare to see ruins.

The number of monks resident in a given monastery is very difficult to ascertain. Monks registered as members may live some distance away and come in only for special occasions. Unregistered monks, especially children, may be in residence but are not counted by the abbot or reported to the Religious Affairs Bureau. Finally, there is a tendency for monastery representatives to exaggerate past figures or round them upward. Thus, the population figures in the table must be considered approximate.

Place names are given in their Pinyin forms, as I do not have reliable Tibetan spellings for all of them. In some cases, I have information that the government contributed funds for repair, but these funds were never sufficient, and the rest had to be raised by the monastery.

Tibetan name	Chinese name	Location	Lineage	Fate of buildings 1950-1976	Subsequent status	Number of monks	Source(s)
Palpung	Babang	Babang township, Dege County	Kagyu	Closed in 1958, except for a handful of monks allowed to remain in residence. Small buildings destroyed, main temple untouched, used by government as offices, granary, clinic, and shop.	Reopened in 1982. Largely restored.	At its height: 1,000. Early 1950s: 500. 1984: 371 registered, 140 in residence, some of whom are transient students.	1
Pewar	Baiya	Babang township, Dege County	Sakya	Small buildings destroyed, main temple untouched.	Restored and expanded.	In 1998: about 20.	1
Gönchen	Gengqing	Dege County seat	Sakya	Completely destroyed in 1967.	Rebuilt in new location. In 1950s: 600.	In 1991: 400.	2
Dzongsar	Zhongsha	Maisu District seat Dege County	Sakya	Completely destroyed in 1959.	Rebuilt.	Before 1950: 100. In 1991: about 70. In 1998: about 20.	1
Dzogchen	Zhuqing	Zhuqing Township, Dege County	Nyingma	Completely destroyed in the late 1950s.	Reopened in 1983 and now mostly rebuilt. The government contributed 20,000 yuan.	In 1950: 1300. In 1988: 200 (from source 3).	1, 2
Derge Barkhang (Printing House)	Dege Yinjing Yuan	Dege County seat		Minor damage.	Restored.		1

Tibetan name	Chinese name	Location	Lineage	Fate of buildings 1950-1976	Subsequent status	Number of monks	Source(s)
Korlondo	Keluotong	Keluotong Township seat, Dege County	Sakya	During the Cultural Revolution, monks and villagers successfully protected the main temple from damage.	Original building in excellent condition.	In 1998: 38.	1
Galen	Galun	Keluotong township, Dege County	Sakya	Interior murals covered with plaster, building undamaged.	In urgent need of conservation and repair.	In 1998: 40.	1
Dodra	Duozha	Babang Township, Dege County	Nyingma	Undamaged.	Restored.	In 1994: 50.	1
Tsatsa	Chacha	Axu Township, Dege County	Kagyu	Undamaged.	In urgent need of conservation and repair.	1950: 439 1988: 232 (from source 3)	1
Dargye	Dajin	Rongbacha Township, Ganzi County	Gelug	Completely destroyed. All books, printing blocks, and statues lost.	Reopened in 1983. The government contributed 530,000 yuan, the rest raised by the abbot. Monk residences and one large temple rebuilt, another temple remains in ruins.	Before 1949: 3700. In 1998: 200.	1
Garze	Ganzi	Ganzi County seat	Gelug	Destroyed during the Cultural Revolution.	All seven temples restored since 1983, paid for in part by 440,000 yuan from the government.	In 1957: 3,300. In 1991: 570.	2

Tibetan name	Chinese name	Location	Lineage	Fate of buildings 1950-1976	Subsequent status	Number of monks	Source(s)
Lhagang	Tagong	Kangding County, Tagong Township	Sakya	Largest temple left standing, but two other temples and peripheral buildings destroyed.	Reopened in 1980. Largest temple repaired, two other temples rebuilt. 260,000 yuan invested by the government.	In 1991: 77 registered, of whom 30 are living on the grounds.	1, 2
Garthar	Huiyuan	Qianning, Dawu County	Gelug	Main temple damaged by earthquakes, used as grain storage during Cultural Revolution.	Reopened in 1982. Main temple repaired.	Before 1949: 500. In 1991: 150 registered, of whom 20 live on the grounds.	2
Nyimtsho	Lingque	Dawu County seat	Gelug	Closed in 1958, used as high school and granary. Damaged by Cultural Revolution and 1981 earthquake.	Reopened in 1981. Government gave 250,000 yuan for repair and to build an irrigation system for the monastery's apple orchard.	Before 1949: 2,000. In 1991: 620 registered, of whom 200 live on the grounds.	2
Tongkor	Donggu	25 km east of Ganzi County seat	Gelug	Damaged by earthquakes.	Reopened in 1982. Government gave 12,000 yuan for repairs. Reconstruction under way in 1991.	Early 1950s: 1,000. In 1991: 300.	2
Mangyal	Manjin	Wentuo Township, Dege County	Bön	Closed during Cultural Revolution. All three original temples survive. One of them dates back to 1700.	Reopened 1982. In 1985 government allocated 15,000 yuan for restoration.	Before 1949: 150. In 1991: 70.	2

Tibetan name	Chinese name	Location	Lineage	Fate of buildings 1950-1976	Subsequent status	Number of monks	Source(s)
Gartok	Gatuo	Hebo, Baiyu County	Nyingma	Most—perhaps all—buildings destroyed.	At least two temples rebuilt.	Early 1950s: 600. 1991: 280.	2, 4
Lithang	Litang	Litang County Seat	Gelug	Destroyed by aerial bombing in 1956. One small original building survived.	Construction of two major temples under way in 1991, work completed by 1999.		1
Rikhu	Riku	Kangding County, Jiagenba Township	Sakya	Sacked during Cultural Revolution, interior badly damaged, exterior left intact. One valuable Tara statue not taken.	Reopened 1976. Repaired late 1990s. In 2000 new statues and murals were being made.	Before 1950: 500. 1976: 50. 2000: 120.	1
Sershul	Shiqu	Shiqu County, Xiqu District	Gelug	All six temples were sacked, but exteriors left standing, interiors only moderately damaged, and a few precious relics not taken.	All original temples renovated and now in use. One large new temple under construction in 2000.	Before 1950:1500 to 1600. 2000: 1300.	1
Minyag Kazhi	Gao'er	Kangding county, near Yajiang County border	Sakya	Partly damaged.	Reopened in 1984.	Before 1966: 500. In 1998: 100.	1

Sources:
1. Personal visit
2. On-site interviews conducted by Wong How Man during his 1991 survey and subsequently published by the China Exploration and Research Society in a report titled "Buddhist Monasteries of Ganzi Tibetan Autonomous Prefecture, Sichuan, China" (1992).
3. *Annals of Dege County* (Sichuan Nationalities Publishing House, 1995).
4. Gyurme Dorje, *Tibet Handbook with Bhutan* (Passport Books, 1997).

House, 77; audience with, 6;
house in Derge, 5; travels of,
145
pigments, 196
prostrations, 178–79
Public Security: monitoring
visiting lama, 2
Purbu Tsering, 61

Qiang, 34
Qiang nationality, 34
Qing Empire, 37

Razat, 4, 31–33, 185
Red Guards, 223
Ren Dekong, 150, 151–54
road construction, 146

Sakya sect, 210–11;
architectural features of
monasteries, 125; Lhagang
Monastery, 44; monasteries
in Derge, 126; Pewar
Monastery's conversion to,
57
Sanday, John, 4, 8–9, 31–33,
50–51, 185
schools in Babang township,
151–52
Serdar, 40
Sershul, 48
Shongshong, 50, 73, 146, 185;
and the Dalai Lama, 28;
childhood, 25–26; devotion
to Pewar Rinpoche, 10; first

meeting with, 7–8; in
Kangding, 82–83; on the
Communist Party, 30;
receiving wages, 180; youth,
26–27
Shu, 34
Sichuan International Cultural
Exchange Center, 76, 109,
187
Sichuan Nationalities Research
Institute, 4
Situ Panchen, 161
Situ Rinpoche, 22, 70, 98, 123,
124, 161, 186; history,
17–18; meeting with, 18–19;
relations with China, 18;
support for Palpung, 20; visit
to Palpung, 18
Songtsen Gampo, 47, 209

Tagong, 44
Tashi Dendrup, 121
Tawu, 38; architecture, 45; as
part of Trehor, 45
Tengyur, 210
Tenzeng Nyima, 49, 92–95,
145, 146, 160–61, 177–78,
185
Thangla Tsewang, 61–62
thanka: description of, 60;
reasons for painting, 60
Tibetan School of Sichuan,
80–81, 89, 148
timber industry, 153, 181;
protected trees, 49

About the Kham Aid Foundation

The Kham Aid Foundation ("KAF") was founded in 1997 by Pamela Logan to support conservation of Tibet's architecture and art. Since then, KAF has developed a broad range of assistance programs focusing on the eastern plateau of Tibet. Nevertheless, KAF is still a small outfit, with one full-time employee in China and one full-time unpaid staffer—Logan herself—in the U.S. Office space is generously provided by the firm of Hines and Jones in Los Angeles.

The Kham Aid Foundation is a California non-profit corporation, and tax-exempt in accord with section 501(c)(3) of the Federal Tax Code.

For more information on the activities of the Kham Aid Foundation, see **www.khamaid.org**

Pamela Logan has been working and traveling on the Tibetan plateau since 1990. She earned her doctorate in aerospace science from Stanford University and has taught engineering at Cal Tech, but has devoted her time for the last decade to the preservation of Tibetan culture. She is the author of *Among Warriors: A Woman Martial Artist in Tibet* (Overlook, 1996; Vintage Books, 1998), a *New York Times* Notable Book. The president of the Kham Aid Foundation, in 1996 she was named "Woman Explorer of the Year" by the Scientific Exploration Society. Her photography has been seen in *National Geographic, Newsweek,* and the *New York Times'* travel section. She has lectured on Tibet extensively, including for the Royal Geographical Society, Asia Society, Explorer's Club, Foreign Correspondents Club of Hong Kong and Beijing, California Institute of Technology, Pacific-Asia Museum, and other organizations. Logan lives in southern California.

Schmitt